As one of the world's longest estab...
and best-known travel brands,
Thomas Cook are the experts in travel.

For more than 135 years our
guidebooks have unlocked the secrets
of destinations around the world,
sharing with travellers a wealth of
experience and a passion for travel.

**Rely on Thomas Cook as your
travelling companion on your next trip
and benefit from our unique heritage.**

Thomas Cook **traveller** guides

IRELAND
Eric and Ruth Bailey

Thomas Cook

Your travelling companion since 1873

Written by Eric and Ruth Bailey, updated by Donna Dailey
Original photography by Michael Short

Published by Thomas Cook Publishing
A division of Thomas Cook Tour Operations Limited
Company registration no. 3772199 England
The Thomas Cook Business Park, Unit 9, Coningsby Road,
Peterborough PE3 8SB, United Kingdom
Email: books@thomascook.com, Tel: +44 (0) 1733 416477
www.thomascookpublishing.com

Produced by Cambridge Publishing Management Limited
Burr Elm Court, Main Street, Caldecote CB23 7NU
www.cambridgepm.co.uk

ISBN: 978-1-84848-543-3

Series Editor: Karen Beaulah
Production/DTP: Steven Collins

Printed and bound in India by Replika Press Pvt Ltd

Cover photography © Riccardo Spila/SIME/4Corners

Contents

Introduction

Ireland means different things to different people, but some things are common to everyone. Everybody remarks on the natural and sincere warmth of the welcome they get from the Irish people. Nobody can fail to appreciate the landscapes and seascapes – sometimes merely pretty, sometimes beautiful, other times spectacular and wild.

The early Christian and prehistoric megaliths, dolmens, round towers and ruins are awe-inspiring, often mysterious. Coming across them casually, sometimes unexpectedly, both in the town and in the countryside, evokes a profound sense of antiquity.

Another thing that cannot go unnoticed in Ireland is that the elements rarely keep still for long. You could stand in one spot watching the changing scene. Blue sky, contrasting sunlight and shadow. Two minutes later, banking clouds, sun in and out. After that, grey streaks the sky – reach for your umbrella. The grey thickens into rolling swathes, almost navy blue, then out comes the sun, and maybe a rainbow. The landscape responds to the fickle weather, bright or hazy, picked out in distant detail, suddenly brooding.

Dublin is a flirtatious city, captivating its visitors. Belfast has dignity. Cork, Galway, Waterford and Limerick all have their own distinctive characters. And everywhere the seafood is sublime. Most visitors enjoy the social life, which takes place to a large extent in the many friendly pubs and bars.

The volume of traffic, particularly in the cities, has increased considerably over the last few years. However, in rural areas a hold-up is as likely to be caused by cows or sheep moving to fresh pastures as by vehicles.

Rolling moorlands in the Wicklow Mountains

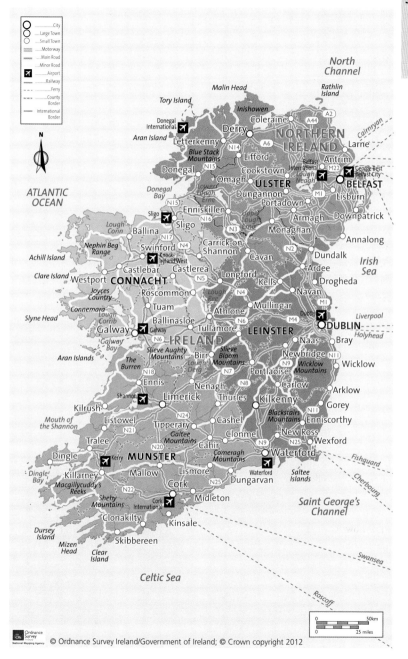

The land

Ireland lies on the continental shelf to the west of the European mainland. In the east it is separated from Britain by the Irish Sea. To the northeast, the North Channel brings Scotland to within 21km (13 miles) of the Antrim coast. To the west lies the vastness of the Atlantic Ocean, while to the south lies St George's Channel.

Two great mountain ranges converge in Ireland. The older Caledonian system, extending from Scandinavia and Scotland to the north and west of Ireland, gives rise to the rugged terrain of Counties Donegal, Galway and Mayo. The younger Armorican system extends from central Europe through Brittany to southwest Ireland, culminating in the 1,041m

Stunning scenery in rural Donegal

(3,415ft)-high Carrauntoohill, the country's highest mountain, in Macgillycuddy's Reeks. Killarney's celebrated 'lakes and fells' are on the eastern slopes of the Reeks.

A narrow belt of lowland crosses the country from the Carlingford Peninsula and the Wicklow Mountains in the east to the Atlantic Ocean in the west, along the Shannon Estuary, Galway Bay, Clew Bay and Donegal Bay. In County Clare, the lowland rises westward, terminating at the magnificent Cliffs of Moher.

The stately 340km (211-mile)-long River Shannon is the largest of Ireland's rivers. Rising in County Leitrim, it opens up into a series of attractive lakes before reaching its broad, indented estuary between Counties Clare and Limerick.

The main eastward-flowing rivers are the Lagan, which runs to the sea at Belfast; the Liffey, with Dublin at its mouth; and the Slaney, which meets the sea at Wexford. In Ulster, the River Erne flows north, opening into Upper and Lower Lough Erne before entering Donegal Bay.

Ireland's climate is legendary, and there is some truth in the joke that observes: 'When you can see the mountain it means it is going to rain; when you cannot see it, it is raining.' In reality, though, the climate is mild and without extremes, due largely to the Gulf Stream, whose relatively warm waters wash Ireland's shores.

The heaviest rainfall is in Donegal, Kerry and Mayo, where it may exceed

A rural homestead with a thatched roof

3,000mm (118in) a year. Eastern Ireland is much drier, with Dublin averaging only 785mm (31in) of rain a year.

Two bonuses, however, arise from Ireland's variable weather: the constantly changing light and verdant vegetation. Though limited, the flora has many interesting features. The lanes of Cork and Kerry, for example, are noted for their profuse fuchsia hedgerows, while an Arctic-alpine flora thrives in The Burren in County Clare.

Among Ireland's 27 mammal species are red deer, pine martens, badgers, hares, otters and stoats. The only reptile is the common lizard. Rivers and lakes are rich in salmon, trout and char, as well as coarse fish. Around 125 species of wild birds breed on the island and more than 250 visiting species have been recorded.

History

About 6000 BC	First visible settlement at Mount Sandel in County Londonderry.
About 3000 BC	Neolithic immigrants introduce agriculture, weaving and pottery, and begin building huge megaliths.
About 600 BC	Celtic invaders arrive; Ireland is divided into provinces.
AD 432	St Patrick arrives to convert the Irish. Some evidence of Christianity before this time.
795	Full-scale invasion by the Vikings.
1014	High King BrianBorú defeats the Vikings at Clontarf, but his murder prevents unification of Ireland.
1169	The Anglo-Norman 'Strongbow' helps Dermot MacMurrough, deposed King of Leinster, to regain his throne.
1172	England's Henry II is made overlord of Ireland, opening the way for the establishment of Anglo-Norman estates.
1366	The Statutes of Kilkenny strictly forbid inter-marriage with the Irish, who are also banned from establishing residences in cities, and make the adoption of Irish names, customs and language illegal.
1534–40	Lord Offaly stages an insurrection after Henry VIII breaks with the Catholic Church; Offaly and five brothers are executed when the insurrection fails.
1541	Henry VIII forces Irish chiefs to surrender their lands.
1558–1603	Elizabeth I tightens the English hold on Ireland and launches the 'Plantation' policy, establishing Protestant English and Scottish settlers on land seized from the native Irish Catholics.

1595–1603	Hugh O'Neill, Earl of Tyrone, leads a rebellion, but is forced to surrender.
1607	O'Neill leads other chiefs in the 'Flight of the Earls' to Europe.
1641	Belief that Charles I of England is a Catholic sympathiser provokes rebellion in Ulster and civil war in England.
1649	Oliver Cromwell invades Ireland after defeating and executing Charles I; thousands of Irish are massacred.
1653	Under the Act of Settlement, Cromwell's opponents have their lands seized.
1689–90	King James II of England flees to Ireland after being deposed. He is defeated by William III at the Battle of the Boyne.
1704	The first of a number of laws to be known as the Penal Code restrict Catholic land owning and subsequently ban Catholics from voting, attending schools, and military service.
1769	Guinness® stout is brewed for the first time.
1775	The American War of Independence promotes unrest in Ireland.
1782	Grattan's Parliament – named after Henry Grattan – persuades the British government that the time has come for Catholic emancipation and Irish independence, but nothing comes of it.
1798	United Irishmen, led by Wolfe Tone, stage an uprising which is crushed.
1800	Ireland becomes part of Britain under the Act of Union.
1829	The Catholic Emancipation Act is passed after Daniel O'Connell, 'The Liberator', gains a seat at Westminster.
1845–8	Ireland's population is reduced by some 2 million as a result of starvation due to potato crop failures and emigration.

1881	Charles Stewart Parnell, Home Rule Party leader, encourages the Irish to defy difficult landlords.
1905–8	The Sinn Fein party is founded after the defeat of two Home Rule bills.
1914	Implementation of Home Rule is postponed because of the outbreak of war.
1916	Easter Rising in Dublin. When the rebellion fails, 16 of its leaders are executed.
1920–21	Fighting breaks out between Britain and Ireland; the Anglo-Irish Treaty creates the Irish Free State. Six counties remain part of Britain.
1922	Republicans reject the treaty. Civil war ensues, ending when Fianna Fáil party founder, Eamonn de Valera, is arrested.
1932	De Valera is elected President of the Irish Free State.
1949	The Republic of Ireland is created.

1967–9	Civil Rights Movement in Northern Ireland leads to marches and attacks by loyalists. A breakdown of order brings in British troops; the IRA re-emerges.
1972	Thirteen unarmed demonstrators are killed by British troops on 30 January – 'Bloody Sunday'. Stormont (parliament) is suspended and Westminster imposes direct rule. Severe emergency laws are enforced as acts of terrorism by all sides continue.
1973	Ireland joins the European Union (EU) – then called the European Economic Community.
1986	Under the Anglo-Irish Agreement, the Republic has more say in Northern affairs.
1994	IRA and some loyalist paramilitary forces announce ceasefire nine months after signing of Downing Street Declaration by Britain and Ireland.
1995	Ban on divorce is lifted in the Republic.

Late 1990s	Ireland's fast-growing economy causes it to be dubbed the 'Celtic Tiger'.
1998	The Good Friday Peace Agreement is signed.
1999–2000	The Northern Ireland Assembly is set up to devolve power to Northern Ireland.
2002	Republic of Ireland adopts the euro as its currency and ratifies the Nice Treaty. The Northern Ireland Assembly is disbanded.
2004	The Irish Government bans smoking in the workplace.
2005	IRA renounces violence and commences decommissioning of arms.
2007	Power-sharing government of republicans and loyalists formed at Stormont. Smoking ban in public places in Northern Ireland.
2008	Ireland's economy officially moves into recession. Irish people reject the Lisbon Treaty, effectively bringing to a halt any major reform of the EU.
2009	Two major loyalist groups in the north announce that they will decommission weapons, 15 years after the IRA declared a ceasefire. Ireland's banking industry in near collapse. The Irish people vote to ratify the Lisbon Treaty in a second referendum.
2010	Dublin is designated a UNESCO City of Literature, one of only four such cities in the world. Policing and justice powers are transferred to the Northern Ireland Assembly. Ireland's economic crisis deepens. The Republic agrees an EU–IMF bailout of 85bn euros.
2011	The ruling Fianna Fáil party loses the general election due to its handling of the economic crisis. Fine Gael and Labour parties form a new coalition government. Enda Kenny is appointed Taoiseach (Prime Minister).

Politics

The contrast between the Republic of Ireland and Northern Ireland is no greater than in the area of governance. The Republic has a stable governmental system whereas in the North the political system is fraught with difficulties.

In the Republic of Ireland, economic stability has led to political stability. The government is a parliamentary democracy with two houses – the Dáil Éireann or House of Representatives and the Seanad Éireann or Senate.

There are 166 elected members of the Dáil, who are elected by a single transferable vote system of proportional representation at least once every five years. The Dáil has the power to pass legislation and to nominate or remove the head of government.

Since the early 1990s, no single party has had a majority in the Dáil, so coalition governments are the norm.

The 60 members of the Senate are nominated by the government or elected by university graduates or town councillors. The Senate has an advisory role including the power to delay legislation and to amend bills proposed by the Dáil.

The head of the government is called the Taoiseach (pronounced 'Tee-shock'). At the time of writing, Enda Kenny holds that position. He is the leader of the centre-right Fine Gael party and his government is a coalition with the centre-left Labour party following an election in March 2011 which saw the former ruling party Fianna Fáil drop dramatically in the polls.

The President is head of state and is elected to a seven-year term; no President can serve more than two terms. The current President is

THOMAS COOK'S IRELAND

After organising an excursion to Liverpool in 1846, Thomas Cook set off for Ireland in 1853. Following some difficulty in obtaining facilities from railway managers, a series of tours was set up by John Mason Cook, Thomas Cook's son.

An office was established in Dublin in 1874, and by the end of the century a special brochure advertised tours to every part of Ireland. At that time there were offices in Dublin, Belfast, Queenstown and Cork. During World War II the Belfast office, which remained open, was involved in the movement of Allied troops.

Michael D Higgins, who lives in Árás an Uachtarán, or House of the President, in Phoenix Park, Dublin.

Despite the relative stability in governments, politicians in Ireland are not the most trusted of citizens. Many former politicians have been involved in political scandals and various levels of skulduggery. Many have got away with bribery and corruption. The state has spent millions on investigations into political corruption in what is euphemistically called a 'tribunal'.

In 1973, Ireland joined the European Union (EU) and has benefited considerably from membership. In 2002, Ireland adopted the euro as its currency and ratified the Nice Treaty at its second attempt.

In the early 1990s, the Irish economy took off. Tax incentives and a large number of highly educated graduates, particularly in IT, made foreign investment particularly attractive, so many multinational companies based their European headquarters in Ireland. The Celtic Tiger was born. It lasted a decade or so, finally collapsing as part of the world recession of 2008. In the same year, much to the new Taoiseach's embarrassment, Irish citizens rejected the Lisbon Treaty, which would have created a political constitution for Europe. The vote was reversed in a second referendum in 2009.

Despite an EU–IMF bailout of 85bn euros in 2010, the Republic faces years of austerity and hardship, with the

The Stormont Parliament Buildings, Belfast

governmental budget and economic recovery its biggest political challenges.

In contrast to the Republic, the governmental situation in Northern Ireland is very complicated.

The two major powers in the North are Sinn Féin and the Democratic Unionists (DUP). These two are at polar ends of the political divide. Despite this, they have formed a power-sharing government in the Northern Ireland Assembly. Political violence has been renounced, although occasional incidents between extremists still make the news. There is still mutual distrust between the two sides but the political landscape has been transformed.

Early history

Prehistory lives on in Ireland today. A prolific heritage of field monuments – stone circles, dolmens, passage graves and Celtic forts – dating from thousands of years BC, provides a source of wonder and meditation. They can be found almost everywhere. Many are signposted, and the visitor casually encounters unspoilt ancient monuments which most countries would greedily exploit.

Visiting some of them may involve a walk through muddy farmland.

Such is the case of the pagan Janus figure, a squat Celtic idol facing both ways in a tiny Fermanagh graveyard on Boa Island. Others, such as the great Newgrange tumulus in Co Meath, are easily accessible and present a sophisticated approach to tourism.

Ancient religious monuments dedicated to the old gods, pagan fertility symbols, final resting places, primitive calendars – the purpose for which these monuments were

Entrance to the Bronze Age Newgrange tomb

Carved figures on White Island combine Christian and pagan features

constructed is often a matter of academic debate.

One of the country's most interesting surviving mounds is at the Hill of Tara in Co Meath, now threatened by the opening of a motorway bypass through its immediate vicinity. Originally including a hill fort and several ring forts, it was the residence of the High Kings of Ireland over many centuries. Visitors can see the entrance to a passage grave where finds included the cremated remains of 40 people, and various utensils, which have been carbon-dated at 1800 BC. Also found was the skeleton of a teenage boy wearing a necklace of amber, jet and bronze. His was the only body not cremated.

Celtic crosses, or high crosses, usually very decorative, stand proudly in churchyards throughout Ireland, dating from the early 12th century onwards, some depicting scenes from the scriptures.

The two-faced, stone-carved Janus figure in Caldragh churchyard, Boa Island, exerts a brooding fascination

Culture

For so long a monoculture of Irish Celts, the country has experienced a wave of immigration that has changed most of its major cities into multi-ethnic societies. The Celtic Tiger economy led to an influx of people looking for work and also saw many native Irish returning to their homeland to take up new opportunities; happily Ireland's delightful traditions still hold sway.

Immigration enriches society in many ways, but brings with it a range of problems. It challenges the 'Ireland of the Welcomes' stereotype, but on the other hand it manifests with African-, Asian- or European-born Irish on the streets of Dublin bedecked in green and celebrating St Patrick's Day. Racial diversity is self-evident in most of Ireland, but in some rural towns there is a very low percentage of ethnic migration and little contact with other races.

The music and literary culture of Ireland has always been strong and important to the Celtic identity. It was not weakened during the time of foreign rule. The Irish language suffered and still struggles to survive, but Anglo-Irish literature flourished,

In Ireland the pub is almost a cultural institution in itself

Beaghmore Stone Circle

with Yeats, Wilde, Shaw and Swift being prime exponents of this genre. Joyce, the most Irish of writers, changed the history of literature.

Irish music has developed a global fan base in the past few decades. The meteoric rise of U2 and other Irish rock and pop artists and the success of *Riverdance* have aided and abetted its increased popularity. Traditional music has also reached new heights, with bands such as The Chieftains, The Clancy Brothers (in the USA) and The Dubliners paving the way.

This has been aided by the mushrooming of the global 'Irish pub' industry and its exploitation of Irish bonhomie and fondness of storytelling. A traditional music session in an Irish pub is one of the major attractions of a visit to Ireland.

Myths and legends

Modern Ireland has moved on from the twee 'leprechaun' stories of the past. You will still find people (tour guides) who will wink at you when you ask them if they believe in the 'little people'. But you are unlikely to get a straight answer when you ask them what they truly believe.

In rural areas, you are more likely to encounter more superstition. You may find older folk who claim to believe in wailing banshees and fairies, but again it is hard to know if they are pulling your leg. In the fields, you do occasionally see fairy rings (circular areas of grass that are darker in colour than the surrounding area due to the growth of certain fungi) that are left untouched by farmers, but mostly belief in this kind of thing is on the wane.

Ghosts are an entirely different matter and many places claim to be haunted. Castles, pubs, houses and hotels are all frequented by disenchanted folk from the world of the spirits. Some of the associated stories have a ring of truth and others less so.

There is no doubt, however, that beneath the surface lurk the remnants of the ancient mythical culture of Ireland. There is an absolute fascination with things out of the ordinary and perhaps this can lead to extraordinary things actually happening.

Storytelling is a national pastime and can feature the most mundane of occurrences. It taps into the Irish love of a story and the reverence for the ancient *seanchai* or storyteller.

Exaggeration lies at the heart of storytelling, and if you have a fantastic story to tell the facts are not as important as the telling. To keep your

A wayside shrine in honour of the Blessed Virgin Mary

attention, a little bit of the supernatural is likely to creep in. And you just won't know how much of it is true.

Religion

Religion no longer plays as major a role in Irish society as it used to. In the Republic of Ireland, although about 98 per cent of the population are registered Catholics, not everyone practises their religion. They are Catholics by name rather than by action.

In times past, the Catholic Church was very powerful in Ireland. But the Church, although still a major landowner, is not the force it once was. Recent scandals have further undermined respect for the Church, and Ireland is now a much more secular country.

In the cities and urban areas in particular, church attendances are on the wane. Not very many go to Mass every Sunday, and if they do it is often for the sake of their children, as they believe bringing their children up with some religion is better than none. Church attendance traditionally swells during the feast days of Christmas and Easter, as more infrequent attenders make the effort.

In Northern Ireland, the situation is different. Religion has long been a means to divide communities and still is to an extent. The Protestant community is in the majority in Northern Ireland.

When you visit Ireland you will see the remnants of the religious society, particularly in rural areas. Marian

ST PATRICK

St Patrick's Day, 17 March, is marked in Ireland, the USA and other parts of the world with parades and cheering crowds. Once, St Patrick's Day in Ireland was a very sombre affair, with the pubs closed and parades of industrial floats. Now it is a great multicultural street festival celebrating the new Ireland. It culminates in a grand parade through the streets of Dublin.

Born in the west of Roman Britain about AD 389, Patrick led a restless life. As a boy he was captured by Irish pirates and taken to Co Antrim, where he was sold into slavery. After six years he escaped, trained as a missionary and returned to Ireland 37 years later. He dedicated the rest of his life – some sources say he reached the age of 104 – to challenging the druids and converting the kings of Ireland to Christianity.

shrines, holy wells and rural churches are dotted throughout the countryside and many are now tourist attractions. Graveyards are filled with majestic ancient Celtic crosses.

As you drive into a small town or village, you are still likely to encounter an unexpected major traffic jam early on a Sunday morning as people go to and from Mass. In April and May, the towns fill up with seven- and eight-year-old children smartly dressed as they make their first Holy Communion.

Pilgrimages are still popular with some of the faithful. Lough Derg in Co Donegal is a place of fasting and penance and has welcomed pilgrims for over 1,000 years. On the last Sunday in July, tens of thousands climb steep Croagh Patrick near Westport in Co Mayo – some of them still do it barefoot.

Festivals and events

Festivals large and small are staged throughout Ireland to celebrate activities, interests and anniversaries ranging from the cultural to the practical, from the commonplace to the bizarre. Whatever the event – whether it is concerned with horses or roses, art or oysters – it will almost certainly involve music, often traditional, and it will definitely be fun.

Please note that dates and locations may change from year to year. Tourist offices will have up-to-date information.

January
Major **horse races** at Gowran Park (Co Kilkenny), Leopardstown (Co Dublin), Naas (Co Kildare) and Thurles (Co Tipperary).

February
Dublin International Film Festival; **The Gathering** – traditional music festival, Killarney, Co Kerry.

March
St Patrick's Day (17 March) celebrated throughout Ireland (parades in Belfast and Dublin), pilgrimages at Cultra, Downpatrick and Newry, all in Co Down; **Ulster National Steeplechase**, Downpatrick, Co Down.

April
Arklow Music Festival, Co Wicklow; **Belfast Film Festival**; **Derry Jazz and**

Big Band Festival, Co Londonderry; **Irish Grand National**, Fairyhouse, Co Meath; **Pan Celtic International Festival**, Carlow.

May
Dublin International Piano Competition; **Cork International Choral Festival**; Dundalk International Maytime Festival, Co Louth; **Bray Jazz Festival**, Co Wicklow; **Fleadh Nua** (traditional music, song and dance), Ennis, Co Clare; **Balmoral Show**, Belfast; **The Cat's Laugh Comedy Festival**, Kilkenny.

June
Bloom Garden Festival, Phoenix Park, Dublin; **Belfast City Carnival**; **Irish Derby**, The Curragh, Co Kildare; **Bloomsday** (16 June), celebration of James Joyce's *Ulysses*, Dublin; **Feis na nGleann** (music, dancing, sport), Ballymena, Co Antrim; AIB **Music Festival** in Great Irish Houses, all Ireland; **Fiddlestone** – Irish fiddlers

gather at Belleek, Co Fermanagh; Listowel **Writers' Week**, Listowel, Co Kerry; Lough Swilly International **Street Performance World Championships**, Cork, Portlaoise and Dublin; **Tope and Whitefish Festival**, Rathmullen, Co Donegal.

July

Chamber Music Festival, Bantry, Co Cork; Bray **Air Display**, Co Wicklow; Cork International **Folk Dance Festival**; Galway **Arts Festival**; **Galway Races**; City of Belfast **Rose Week**; **Lughnara Medieval Fair**, Carrickfergus, Co Antrim; **Battle of the Boyne Commemoration** (Orangemen's Day – 12 July), Northern Ireland; **Oxegen Rock & Roll Weekend**, Punchestown, Co Kildare; **Yeats International Summer School**, Co Sligo.

August

Ancient Order of Hibernians' Parade, Co Londonderry; Connemara **Pony Show**, Co Galway; **Dun Laoghaire Festival of World Cultures**, Co Dublin; Kilkenny **Arts Week**; O'Carolan **Harp and Traditional Music Festival**, Keadue, Co Roscommon; **Oul' Lammas Fair**, Ballycastle, Co Antrim; **Heavy Horse and Vintage Vehicle Show**, Ballycastle, Co Antrim; **Puck Fair**, Killorglin, Co Kerry; **Relief of Derry Celebrations** – largest of all the loyal order parades, commemorating siege of 1688–9; **Rose of Tralee International Festival**, Co Kerry; Rosscarbery **Horse Fair**, Co Cork.

September

Matchmaking Festival, Lisdoonvarna, Co Clare; **Opera** – Northern Ireland Autumn Season, Grand Opera House, Belfast; Waterford **International Festival of Light Opera**.

October

Ballinasloe International **Horse Fair and Festival** – one of Europe's largest horse fairs, Co Galway; Cork International **Film and Jazz Festivals**; **Dublin City Marathon**; Kinsale International **Gourmet Festival**, Kinsale, Co Cork; Sligo's world-renowned **Live World Music Festival**; Wexford **Festival of Opera**; **Belfast Festival** – music, from classical to jazz, as well as drama, opera and cinema in and around Queen's University.

November

Bard of Armagh Festival, Armagh, Co Armagh.

December

Christmas horse racing, Leopardstown, Co Dublin; **Wren Boys Festivals** – ancient tradition of 'hunting the wren', possibly originating from the tale of the wren that betrayed St Stephen's location when hiding from his enemies, throughout the country, but especially in Carrigaline, Co Cork; **National Craft & Design Fair**, RDS Dublin; **New Year's Eve Fireworks** over the Liffey, Dublin.

Impressions

Long gone are the days of cute, barefoot redheads bringing turf for the fire in straw baskets on the donkey's back. Ireland's modern infrastructure makes visiting a pleasure, and the variety of lifestyles you will encounter on a trip by road or rail around the country will amuse and delight. The Irish may all have Wi-Fi, communicate by text and tweet at one another, but they can still find room to pass the time of day with anyone perceptive enough to get off the beaten track and find out what life in Ireland is really all about.

The regions

Ireland's ancient provinces – Ulster, Munster, Leinster and Connacht – roughly divide the country into north, south, east and west.

Ulster is an unbelievably beautiful region. North of Belfast, the Antrim Coast Road, leading to the Giant's Causeway, is unquestionably one of the world's most beautiful coastal routes, presenting a kaleidoscope of picturesque glens, villages and fishing harbours. For mountain lovers there are the Mountains of Mourne, sweeping down to the sea in Co Down, and the Sperrins in Co Tyrone. The Fermanagh lakelands are a mecca for boaters and anglers.

Munster extends southwards from Galway Bay to Mizen Head and the island of Cape Clear, and eastwards to Waterford. Soaring cliffs punctuate a coastline of rocky coves and soft, sandy beaches. Here are the ancient places: Viking Limerick and Waterford; the forts of the Dingle Peninsula; and the legendary Rock of Cashel.

Leinster stretches from the border of Ulster south to Co Wexford, and from the Irish Sea to the River Shannon. Here the clan rulers built the great burial mound at Newgrange, and later the High Kings of Ireland ruled from the Hill of Tara. Brian Ború defeated the Vikings at Clontarf, near Dublin, in 1014, and in 1690 William of Orange's victory at the Battle of the Boyne assured another two centuries of Protestant domination.

Connacht, the far west of Ireland, is a land of wide horizons with mountains brooding over the ever-changing Atlantic Ocean on one side and the fertile plains of the Shannon Valley on the other. To the south, medieval Galway City gazes out towards the Aran Islands, and in the north Benbulben dominates Sligo and the landscapes that inspired W B Yeats.

The border

The border between the Republic and Northern Ireland, created in 1921 by

Britain's Government of Ireland Act, loops from the western shore of Lough Foyle to Carlingford Lough, just south of Newry, Co Down.

Under the Act, six of Ulster's nine counties – Antrim, Armagh, Down, Fermanagh, Londonderry and Tyrone – were retained as part of the United Kingdom. Cavan, Donegal and Monaghan, part of the Republic, are the remaining counties.

The border left a number of communities effectively straddling two jurisdictions – no problem during peaceful times (apart from creating opportunities for smuggling), but a security hazard when violence arose.

Now the border stands as a symbol of a divided Ireland, and it underscores the ambivalence implied in the North by the question, 'Are you British or are you Irish?' The people of Northern Ireland can choose between an Irish or British passport – many pragmatists carry both. The removal of customs and immigration barriers in the European Union has effectively removed frontiers between member states, but has made little difference to the mental divide between north and south in Ireland.

In terms of everyday travel, however, the border has never been a truly formidable frontier. Even at the height of the Troubles, when British Army patrols were much in evidence and drivers had to zigzag through barbed-wire barriers, the business of passing from one country to another was

Hay bales, Co Wicklow

completed with little of the formality found in other parts of the world.

The casual nature of the border is underscored by the Shannon–Erne Waterway, which traverses Counties Leitrim, Cavan and Fermanagh, to link the Rivers Shannon and Erne. Opened in 1993, the restored waterway flits back and forth across the border – and is itself the border in some places – but nowhere along its 63km (39-mile) length is there a checkpoint or customs post; instead, the waterway is occupied only by boats and pleasure cruisers.

Lifestyle and etiquette

In contrast to the quiet countryside, Ireland's largest cities are as busy and bustling as anywhere else in Europe. Despite this, you are still likely to strike up a conversation with a stranger at any moment. The art of conversation is not dead yet. A modern phrase sums up

Charming, isolated churches are a feature of the Irish countryside

perfectly a lifestyle which has prevailed in rural Ireland since the first Celtic herdsman reclined on the turf with a happy sigh. The phrase is 'laid-back'.

Life passes at a slower pace and there is a more relaxed attitude to appointments at specific times. If you arrange to meet at 7pm, then this could mean any time from 6pm to 8pm.

A conversation struck up with a fellow passenger on a bus can have either or both of you missing the stop. A visit to the pub can extend well beyond the limit you set yourself, for there is no such thing in Ireland as a quick drink. Warmly, easily, you are drawn into the conversation, questioned but not cross-examined, listened to with courtesy and humour.

The basic rule for visitors is: 'Be garrulous.' When you are addressed, do reply, and fully. Better still, get in first with a greeting and a comment on the weather. Then your conversation could ebb and flow over all manner of subjects from sports to religion and politics. Opinions often may seem fervent and passionate and then be forgotten shortly after. It is the act of conversing rather than the subject that is most important.

For an up-to-date and readable guide to lifestyle and etiquette, see Patricia Levy's *Culture Shock! Ireland.*

Getting there

By air

There are five major international airports in Ireland: Shannon, Dublin, Cork, Knock, and Belfast International at Aldergrove.

A number of airlines fly direct to Dublin, Shannon and Belfast from the USA, including the national carrier **Aer Lingus** (*www.aerlingus.com*) and **Delta Airlines** (*www.delta.com*). Flying via London gives travellers from the USA and Canada a wider choice. As yet there are no direct flights to Ireland from Australia or New Zealand, and any such journey requires a transfer in London.

Dublin Airport has good European connections. Aer Lingus, British Airways, British Midland and Ryanair are the main carriers on routes between the UK and Ireland, while Aer Lingus, Ryanair and other airlines serve major European cities.

Cork Airport has direct flights to Dublin, London and limited continental destinations, with good connecting international flights through Dublin.

Knock International Airport, Charlestown, Co Mayo, owes its existence to a local priest, who campaigned for years for an airport to serve the pilgrims who flock to the nearby village where the Virgin Mary was apparently sighted in 1879. The airport has scheduled services from Britain, as well as international charter flights, and serves the west and northwest.

Belfast is served by two airports. Belfast International at Aldergrove, the principal gateway, is 30km (19 miles) from the city centre, but the motorway link is excellent. British Airways and British Midland both run shuttle services between Aldergrove and London Heathrow and have connections with other major British cities. easyJet has flights to London's Gatwick, Luton and Stansted Airports, and to other European cities. Travellers from North America on scheduled flights are usually routed through London or Shannon, but Continental Airlines flies directly from the USA to Belfast.

George Best Belfast City Airport, only 7km (4 miles) from the city centre, receives flights from London's Heathrow, Stansted, Gatwick and Luton Airports and from other UK provincial airports. (*See* Arriving *pp174–5.*)

By sea

Some of the major cruise lines call at Cobh, Co Cork. However, travel by sea nowadays tends to be a crossing by car ferry from Britain or France.

All major routes to the Republic, apart from Liverpool to Dublin, start in Wales: Holyhead for Dublin and Dun Laoghaire; Fishguard for Rosslare; and Pembroke for Rosslare.

Northern Ireland is served from the Scottish ports of Cairnryan (to Larne) and Stranraer (to Belfast), and from Liverpool (to Belfast). There are also services to Rosslare from Cherbourg and Roscoff, and also to Cork from Roscoff. (*See* Arriving *p175.*)

Moorings on the River Shannon

Traditional music sessions are a highlight

Getting around

Ireland is a small country (though probably much larger than most visitors expect) and connections are generally good either by road, rail or by ferry.

By bus

Long-distance services are operated by Bus Éireann in the Republic and Ulsterbus in Northern Ireland. Both offer a reasonably efficient and inexpensive method of travel, especially in those areas that are infrequently serviced (or in many cases not served at all) by rail. On the whole, city bus services, particularly in Dublin and Belfast, are excellent.

It is possible to travel between Britain and Ireland by bus – although this may not be the quickest way, it is certainly economical. Services are operated by **Eurolines**, based in Britain (*tel: (08717) 818181; www.eurolines.com*).

By car

This is the best way of getting around Ireland. Roads are generally good – and getting better – on both sides of the border. The old image of the Irish road full of potholes has long since given way to a modern experience as many improvement schemes, often funded by the European Union, speed ahead.

By rail

Rail services in the Republic are operated by the state-owned Irish Rail (Iarnród Éireann). Trains are comfortable and generally reliable and the fares reasonable. There are two classes of travel: standard (2nd class) and Citygold (1st class). Most major towns and ports are easily reached from Dublin, but there are large gaps in the system, especially in the northwest.

Northern Ireland Railways, also state-owned, operates between Belfast and Londonderry, Larne, Bangor and Dublin. The Enterprise Service Express travels non-stop between Belfast and Dublin in approximately two hours. There are eight trains a day in each direction Monday to Saturday, with five on Sunday.

Further details on rail services can be obtained from the Thomas Cook *European Timetable*, published monthly. (*See* Public transport *pp185–6.*)

A horse-cart view of the country reflects its easy-going pace of life

Leinster

Leinster is a province of varied and lovely scenery, with fascinating bogland, fish-filled lakes, the River Shannon, nature reserves, sandy beaches, stately homes and castles. There are more counties here than in the other three provinces – 12 of the 32 – plus the Republic's capital, Dublin.

Dublin City

Set along the River Liffey, the Republic's lively capital city is the first stop for many visitors and provides a fine introduction to Ireland. It is the seat of government, the main business and financial centre, and home to the nation's leading university, Trinity College. Some of the country's finest arts and cultural institutions can be found here, from the National Museum of Ireland to the National Gallery, as well as two great cathedrals and such historic treasures as Dublin Castle and the *Book of Kells*. Handsome Georgian squares, colourful St Stephen's Green, good restaurants and great nightlife make it a favourite destination.

Abbey Theatre

Founded in 1904 by W B Yeats and friends for the performance of plays by, and about, the Irish, the Abbey has premiered the works of Yeats, Synge, Shaw, O'Casey and others.

It incorporates the smaller Peacock Theatre, which features more contemporary works.
Lower Abbey St, Dublin 1. Tel: (01) 878 7222. www.abbeytheatre.ie

Bank of Ireland

This magnificent 18th-century building, with its huge multicoloured porticoes and sculptured figures, was originally designed as the Irish Parliament House. The former House of Lords can be seen on a tour (*Tue 10.30am, 11.30am & 1.45pm*). *2 College Green, Dublin 2. Tel: (01) 677*

The 18th-century building of the Bank of Ireland

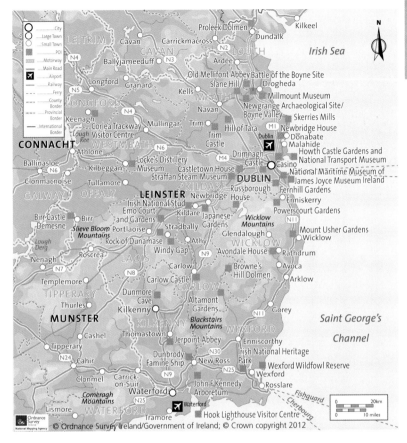

© Ordnance Survey Ireland/Government of Ireland; © Crown copyright 2012

6801. Open: Mon–Fri 10am–4pm
(Thur until 5pm). Free admission.
Arts centre open: Tue–Fri 10am–4pm.
Admission charge.

Chester Beatty Library and Gallery of Oriental Art

Donated to the country by Sir Alfred
Chester Beatty (1875–1968), exhibits
date from 2700 BC and include
illustrated medieval manuscripts and
religious texts ranging from biblical
papyri to Persian Korans, prints, wall
hangings and oriental artefacts.
The Clocktower Building, Dublin Castle.
Tel: (01) 407 0750. www.cbl.ie. Open:
May–Sept Mon–Fri 10am–5pm, Sat
11am–5pm, Sun 1–5pm; Oct–Apr
Tue–Fri 10am–5pm, Sat 11am–5pm,
Sun 1–5pm. Free admission.

Christ Church Cathedral

The Church of Ireland (Anglican)
cathedral is Dublin's oldest building

Sumptuous furnishings for the State Drawing Rooms in Dublin Castle

and was founded in 1038 by Sitric Silkenbeard, King of the Dublin Norsemen, who built a simple wooden church here. It was later rebuilt in stone by Richard de Clare, Earl of Pembroke (known as Strongbow), in 1169. There is a monument to Strongbow in the nave. The 12th-century crypt contains interesting relics including 17th-century punishment stocks which once stood in the churchyard.
Christchurch Place, Dublin 8.
Tel: (01) 677 8099. www.cccdub.ie.
Open: Apr, May, Sept & Oct Mon–Sat
9.30am–6pm, Sun 12.30–2.30pm;
Jun–Aug Mon–Sat 9.30am–7pm, Sun
12.30–2.30pm & 4.30–6pm; Nov–Mar
Mon–Sat 9.30am–5pm, Sun
12.30–2.30pm. Admission charge.

City Hall

Recently beautifully restored and opened to the public, City Hall was built between 1769 and 1779 as the Royal Exchange. It was the scene of the Irish Volunteer rallies in the 1780s, and government troops used it as a barracks and torture chamber during the 1798 rebellion. It has a beautiful domed entrance hall. A multimedia exhibition 'The Story of the Capital' traces the evolution of the capital.
Dame St, Dublin 2. Tel: (01) 222 2204.
www.dublincity.ie/dublincityhall.
Open: Mon–Sat 10am–5.15pm.
Admission charge for exhibition; free admission to Rotunda.

Custom House

This 18th-century building, designed by James Gandon, was severely damaged by fire in 1921 (*see p46*). Extensive restoration work was finally completed in 1991. The visitor centre features a Gandon museum.
Custom House Quay, Dublin 1.
Tel: (01) 888 2538. Open: mid-Mar–Oct
Mon–Fri 10am–12.30pm, Sat & Sun
2–5pm; Nov–mid-Mar Wed–Fri
10am–12.30pm, Sat & Sun 2–5pm.
Admission charge.

Dublin Castle

Built in the early 13th century, only one of the four Norman towers – the Record Tower – survives. Presidents of Ireland have been inaugurated in lofty St Patrick's Hall since 1938, and foreign dignitaries are hosted in the elegant State Apartments (*see p44*). In the grounds of the castle is the site of the *dubh linn* or 'black pool' that gave the city its name. It is now marked by a small fountain.
Dame St, Dublin 2. Tel: (01) 645 8813.
www.dublincastle.ie. Open: Mon–Sat

10am–4.45pm, Sun & public holidays noon–4.45pm. Times may vary because of state functions. Admission charge.

Dublinia and the Viking World
The story of Viking Dublin is told with all the relevant smells and noises. Good fun, plus you can climb St Michael's Tower and look out over the city. *St Michael's Hill, Dublin 8. Tel: (01) 679 4611. www.dublinia.ie.*

Open: daily 10am–5pm. Admission charge.

Dublin Writers' Museum
The full glory of this fine Georgian building can be best appreciated from the writers' gallery on the first floor. A taped tour takes the visitor through the history of Irish literature on the ground floor. Exhibits include authors' memorabilia, first editions and

Dublin

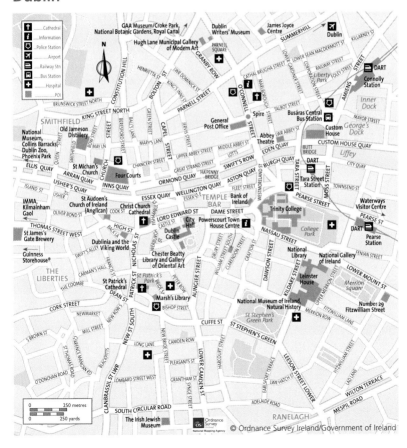

photographs. There is also a modern writers' picture gallery, Zen garden, bookshop and café.

18 Parnell Square North, Dublin 1. Tel: (01) 872 2077. www.writers museum.com. Open: Mon–Sat 10am–5pm, Sun & public holidays 11am–5pm. Admission charge.

Dublin Zoo

Opened to the public in 1840, this is one of the few zoos where lions have bred in captivity, one achieving worldwide fame as the MGM film lion. It is a spacious zoo with a large collection of wild animals and birds, many rare and endangered species, from all around the world. The African Plains exhibit is particularly popular.

Phoenix Park, Dublin 8. Tel: (01) 474 8900. www.dublinzoo.ie. Open: daily 9.30am–6pm; winter daily until dusk. Admission charge.

Four Courts

Architect James Gandon produced a masterpiece with this building. Opened in 1802, it now houses the law courts of Chancery, King's Bench, Exchequer and Common Pleas.

Inns Quay, Dublin 7. Tel: (01) 888 6000. Open: Mon–Fri 11am–1pm & 2–4pm. Free admission.

GAA Museum/Croke Park

GAA stands for Gaelic Athletic Association and Croke Park is home to the two unique national games of Ireland, hurling and Gaelic football.

Gas lamp, Dublin

The museum takes you through the history of the sports.

Croke Park, Dublin 3. Tel: (01) 819 2323. www.crokepark.ie/GAA-Museum. Open: Jul & Aug Mon–Sat 9.30am–6pm, Sun 10.30am–5pm; Sept–Jun Mon–Sat 9.30am–5pm, Sun 10.30am–5pm. Admission charge.

General Post Office

The imposing GPO building, with its Ionic portico and fluted pillars, was completed in 1818 and virtually destroyed in the Easter Rising (*see p46*). It reopened in 1929. Inside is a bronze statue of Cúchulainn, leader of the Red Branch Knights in Irish mythology.

O'Connell St, Dublin 1. Tel: (01) 705 7000. Open: Mon–Sat 8am–8pm, Sun & public holidays 10am–6.30pm. Free admission.

Guinness Storehouse®

The Guinness Storehouse® is an outstanding exhibition set out over six floors, taking the visitor through the production of Guinness® from grain to final product. Enjoy your free pint in the Gravity Bar at the very top, which has a wonderful 360-degree view over the city.
St James's Gate, Dublin 8. Tel: (01) 408 4800. www.guinnessstorehouse.com. Open: daily 9.30am–5pm. Admission charge (10 per cent discount if booked online).

Hugh Lane Municipal Gallery of Modern Art

This gallery, founded by Sir Hugh Lane, opened in 1930. He bequeathed his collection of mainly Impressionist pictures to the nation. This gift is joined by other works of 20th-century Irish and international art and an excellent stained-glass gallery. The London studio of artist Francis Bacon was given to the gallery in 2001 and is reconstructed here in its entirety.
Charlemont House, Parnell Square North, Dublin 1. Tel: (01) 222 5550. www.hughlane.ie. Open: Tue–Thur 10am–6pm, Fri & Sat 10am–5pm, Sun 11am–5pm. Free admission.

IMMA

The Irish Museum of Modern Art (IMMA) is housed in the former Kilmainham Royal Hospital, which is Ireland's only surviving fully classical 17th-century building. It was designed by William Robinson in the 1680s to house retired and disabled soldiers. It officially passed to the Irish Free State in 1922. It now houses the IMMA, whose excellent displays of international art include works by Picasso and Irish art of the 20th century. In the grounds are two cemeteries: one is believed to contain the body of Irish patriot Robert Emmet, who led the 1803 rising and was executed. British soldiers who died in the 1916 Easter Rising occupy the other, along with army pensioners.
Military Rd, Dublin 8. Tel: (01) 612 9900. www.imma.ie. Museum open: Tue–Sat 10am–5.30pm (Wed from 10.30am), Sun & public holidays noon–5.30pm. Free admission.

The Irish Jewish Museum

One of the last remnants of the thriving Jewish community that lived in the Portobello area of Dublin. This clunky little museum, which was once a synagogue, provides a fascinating insight into the lives of the people who resided here. Particularly gripping is the

KILMAINHAM'S INMATES

Eamonn de Valera, born in New York of Irish ancestry, strongly influenced Irish politics over a long period. His spell in gaol was for his part in the 1916 Easter Rising; he was released in 1924 and went on to be leader of Fianna Fáil, Taoiseach and, later, President. He opened the gaol as a museum in 1966. Leaders of the Easter Rising were executed at the gaol, among them Con Colbert, Pádraic Pearse and James Connolly.

The Dáil building

story told in old letters, posters and newspaper articles of the Irish attitude to Jews and the plight of European Jews during World War II.
3–4 Walworth St, Dublin 8. Tel: (01) 490 1857. Open: May–Sept Sun– Thur 11am–3.30pm; Oct–Apr Sun 10.30am–2.30pm. Free admission, but donations welcome.

James Joyce Centre
The literary display in this impressive Georgian house includes biographies of characters from *Ulysses* based on Dublin people whom Joyce knew. Walking tours of the author's Dublin are organised. The centre is run by the Joyce family.
35 North Great Georges St, Dublin 1. Tel: (01) 878 8547. www.jamesjoyce.ie. Open: Apr–Sept Mon–Sat 10am–5pm, Sun noon–5pm; Oct–Mar Tue–Sat 10am–5pm, Sun noon–5pm. Admission charge.

Kilmainham Gaol
History covering an eventful century and a half is almost tangible at Kilmainham Gaol, erected in 1796. Now a museum with a fascinating audiovisual presentation pinpointing Irish political and penal history from the 1780s to the 1920s, the old gaol still presents a chilling atmosphere. Executions were conducted here after the Easter Rising in 1916.
Kilmainham, Dublin 8. Tel: (01) 453 5984. Open: Apr–Sept daily 9.30am–6pm; Oct–Mar Mon–Sat 9.30am–5.30pm, Sun 10am–6pm. Admission charge.

Leinster House
The Dáil (lower house) and Seanad (Senate) of the Irish Parliament convene in this lavish building, which was constructed in 1745 as the town house of the Dukes of Leinster. Tours of the government buildings take place every Saturday.
Kildare St, Dublin 2. Tel: (01) 618 3000. http://www.oireachtas.ie. Tours: by prior arrangement.

Marsh's Library
Dating from 1701, this is Ireland's oldest public library. Inside are 'cages' in which readers were locked to prevent the theft of books.
St Patrick's Close, Dublin 8. Tel: (01) 454 3511. www.marshlibrary.ie. Open: Mon & Wed–Fri 9.30am–1pm & 2–5pm, Sat 10am–1pm. Admission charge.

James Joyce

James Joyce, one of Ireland's greatest writers, spent most of his life outside the country, but he wrote only about Dublin and Dubliners. He knew the city so well and used its detail so minutely in his works, that it was claimed (supposedly by Joyce himself) that if Dublin were to be totally destroyed, his novel *Ulysses* could be used as a blueprint to rebuild it. Born in 1882 at 41 Brighton Square, in Rathgar, 5km (3 miles) from the city centre, Joyce lived at more than 20 other addresses before leaving Dublin at the age of 22. After that he wrote about the city as he travelled abroad.

Bust of James Joyce on St Stephen's Green, Dublin

Between 1893 and 1898 he attended Belvedere College in Great Denmark Street before studying at University College Dublin. At 35 North Great Georges Street is the James Joyce Centre (*see p34*), whose library and archives attract serious students of the writer and his work.

Every year, 16 June – the day on which the whole action of *Ulysses* takes place – sees special Bloomsday events throughout the city and at other places mentioned in the novel where Leopold Bloom or Stephen Dedalus spend part of their day. Many fans of the book take a pilgrimage through the sites mentioned in it.

The day starts at the James Joyce tower in Sandycove (use the DART) where the first scenes of the book take place.

Lunchtime is when fans flock to Davy Byrne's pub on Duke Street where Bloom famously lunched on a glass of Burgundy and a Gorgonzola sandwich.

Sandymount Strand, a 5km (3-mile) beach between Ringsend and Booterstown, is another *Ulysses* setting and was a favourite spot with Joyce and his wife, Nora Barnacle.

National Botanic Gardens

Twenty thousand different plant species are set in 19.5 hectares (48 acres) of rock, herb and rose gardens and herbaceous borders, and in the superb mid-19th-century glasshouses, designed and built by Richard Turner. The gardens, beside the River Tolka, date from 1795.

Glasnevin, Dublin 9. Tel: (01) 804 0300. www.botanicgardens.ie. Open: Mar–Oct Mon–Fri 9am–5pm, Sat & Sun 10am–6pm; Nov–Feb daily 9am–4.30pm. Free admission.

National Gallery of Ireland

The gallery houses Ireland's foremost collection of paintings, including works by Rembrandt, Reynolds, El Greco and Goya. Every major European school of painting is represented among its thousands of exhibits. Irish painters are strongly represented, with works by George Barrett, Francis Danby, James Latham and Jack B Yeats. The Millennium Wing is an architectural delight and provides increased exhibition space and excellent facilities.

The National Museum of Ireland at Collins Barracks is home to a range of objects

Clare St, Merrion Square West, Dublin 2. Tel: (01) 661 5133. www.nationalgallery.ie. Open: Mon–Sat 9.30am–5.30pm (Thur until 8.30pm), Sun noon–5.30pm. Tours available. Free admission.

National Library

This treasure house of information about Ireland has many books, including first editions, complete files of Irish magazines and newspapers, maps, prints, drawings and photographs. Tickets are issued for reading the books.

Kildare St, Dublin 2. Tel: (01) 603 0200. www.nli.ie. Open: Mon–Wed 9.30am–7.45pm, Thur & Fri 9.30am–4.45pm, Sat 9.30am–12.45pm. Free admission.

National Museum of Ireland, Collins Barracks

Collins Barracks, the oldest military barracks in Europe, is now the site of a sprawling museum of the decorative arts and of economic, social, political and military history of Ireland. Displays range from weapons to furniture, silver, glassware, costumes and textiles.

Collins Barracks, Benburb St, Dublin 7. Tel: (01) 677 7444. www.museum.ie. Open: Tue–Sat 10am–5pm, Sun 2–5pm. Free admission.

National Museum of Ireland, Natural History

Displays in this venerable building date from its opening in 1857, and include giant deer skeletons and other

taxonomic specimens of Ireland's wildlife and landscape.
Merrion St, Dublin 2. Tel: (01) 677 7444. www.museum.ie. Open: Tue–Sat 10am–5pm, Sun 2–5pm. Free admission.

Number 29 Fitzwilliam Street
A beautifully restored Georgian house, filled with original furnishings and household items from the National Museum's collection. There are details about the daily lives of the family and their servants, who originally lived there. An hour well spent.
29 Fitzwilliam St, Dublin 2. Tel: (01) 702 6165. www.esb.ie/numbertwentynine. Open: Tue–Sat 10am–5pm, Sun noon–5pm. Admission charge.

The Old Jameson Distillery
The Jameson Distillery was converted into the head offices of Irish Distillers after it closed in 1972. The old distillery can be visited on a guided tour. There are working models of the distilling process, an audiovisual presentation on Irish whiskey, and a sampling of the goods in the Jameson bar afterwards.
Bow St, Smithfield Village, Dublin 7. Tel: (01) 807 2348. www.jamesonwhiskey.ie. Open: daily 10am–6pm. Last tour 5.15pm. Admission charge.

Phoenix Park
One of the largest enclosed public parks in the world with 710 hectares (1,754 acres), Phoenix Park was laid out in the 18th century. Its name actually derives from *fionn uisce* and means

The Old Jameson Distillery in Smithfield Village

'clear water'. It contains gardens, woods, a herd of deer and the Dublin Zoo (*see p32*), with space for playing sports. The residences of the Irish President and the US ambassador, and the headquarters of the Garda (police), with the restored Ashtown Castle and a visitor centre, are also in the park.
West of Heuston Station, Dublin 8. Open: daily 24 hrs. Visitor centre: tel: (01) 677 0095. www.phoenixpark.ie. Open: Mar–Oct daily 10am–6pm; Nov–Feb Wed–Sun 9.30am–5.30pm. Free admission.

Powerscourt Town House Centre
Renovated in the 1980s into a precinct of select shops, cafés, craft shops and boutiques, these former wholesale textile company's premises were originally built between 1771 and 1774 as the town mansion of the Powerscourt family.
William St South, Dublin 2. Tel: (01) 679 4144. www.powerscourtcentre.ie. Open: Mon–Fri 10am–6pm (Thur until 8pm), Sat 9am–6pm, Sun noon–6pm.

Literary Ireland

The literary heritage of Ireland is quite extraordinary for the size of the island. There is a culture of literary excellence that stems from the ancient storyteller or *seanchai* who used to travel from house to house telling tales in front of the hearth. Since that time, four Nobel prizes for literature have been awarded to Irish writers – William Butler (W B) Yeats, George Bernard Shaw, Samuel Beckett and Seamus Heaney – and many fine contemporary writers have followed in the footsteps of these literary greats.

James Joyce's masterpiece *Ulysses* is based on a day in 1904 in Dublin, and he famously claimed that the city could be rebuilt from his novel if it were ever destroyed. You can follow the trail of the main character, Leopold Bloom, since many of the places that feature in the book still exist. Other famous Dublin writers include Oscar Wilde, Jonathan Swift (*Gulliver's Travels*),

Oscar Wilde statue in Merrion Square

He passed, dallying, the windows of Brown Thomas, silk mercers.

Commemorative plaque to James Joyce

Bram Stoker (*Dracula*), J M Synge, Maeve Binchy, Roddy Doyle (*The Commitments*) and the irreverent Brendan Behan. Famous blow-ins not born in Dublin include Flann O'Brien and the poet Patrick Kavanagh. Indeed, so many writers hailed from Dublin or spent their life there that there is now a writers' museum in the city (*see pp31–2*).

Some of these writers had more-than-colourful characters and used to frequent a number of famous Dublin pubs. There is a literary tour that takes in many of their favourite drinking holes.

There are many other areas of Ireland that have inspired famous writers. J M Synge was prompted by his visit to the Aran Islands to write his famous play *Playboy of the Western World*. Life has changed on the islands since then, but not by much.

On the mainland, you can drive through Yeats country in County Sligo and visit his grave at Drumcliff. And further south, Limerick city was unfavourably depicted in the bestseller *Angela's Ashes* by Frank McCourt.

Famous writers from Northern Ireland include Seamus Heaney, Louis MacNeice, C S Lewis, Bernard McLaverty and Brian Moore.

Writing in Irish has undergone a revival with the increasing popularity of the language. Some of the finer exponents include Cathal Ó Searcaigh, Nuala Ni Domhnaill, Michael O Siadhail and Gabriel Rosenstock.

Detailed woodcarving on St Michan's organ, which dates from around 1725

Royal Canal

A pleasant waterway with more than 11km (7 miles) of towpath winding through northern Dublin, the Royal Canal never reached its full potential as a cargo-carrying connection between the Liffey and the Shannon; the Grand Canal, passing through the city's southern suburbs, was already fulfilling that role. Long John Binns, a shoemaker, founded the Royal as a rival waterway in 1789. It lost money from the start, though the canal endures to this day as a leisure attraction.

St Audoen's Church of Ireland (Anglican)

One of the oldest churches in Dublin, near a preserved stretch of the city wall and minus much of its roof, St Audoen's is dated variously from AD 650 to 1169. A pre-Norse church of St Columcille once stood on the site. The tower contains three bells, cast in 1423, said to be the oldest in Ireland. In the porch is an early Christian gravestone, known as the 'Lucky Stone', which has been kept at the church since before 1309.

Next door to St Audoen's Church of Ireland is the Roman Catholic church of the same name, dating from the 1840s. *High St, Dublin 8. Visitor centre tel: (01) 677 0088. Open: late Apr–late Oct daily 9.30am–5.30pm. Free admission.*

St Michan's Church

The original 1095 Danish church was almost completely rebuilt in the 1680s and restored in the 19th century. The finely carved 18th-century organ in the Anglican church is believed to have been played by Handel while composing *The Messiah* in the year which saw its first public performance at Neale's New Music Hall in Fishamble Street. Probably the main 'attraction' at St Michan's is a tour of the vaults, where a number of perfectly preserved mummies, some from the 17th century, can be viewed (*see p47*). *Lower Church St, Dublin 8. Tel: (01) 872 4154. Open: Mar–Oct Mon–Fri 10am–12.45pm & 2–4.45pm, Sat 10am–12.45pm; Nov–Mar Mon–Fri 12.30–3.30pm, Sat 10am–12.45pm. Admission charge.*

St Patrick's Cathedral

St Patrick is said to have baptised converts to the Christian faith in a well which once existed adjacent to the present National Cathedral of the Church of Ireland. Because of the sacred association with St Patrick, a church has stood here since the 5th century. A Norman church was built on the site in 1191, and rebuilding took place in the first half of the 13th century, resulting in the magnificent edifice which exists today. Jonathan Swift, Dean of St Patrick's for more than 30 years, is buried in the nave, and there is a marble bust of him in the south aisle (*see p44*).

St Patrick's Close, Dublin 8. Tel: (01) 453 9472. www.stpatrickscathedral.ie. Open: Mar–Oct Mon–Fri 9am–5pm, Sat 9am–6pm, Sun 9–10.30am, 12.30– 2.30pm & 4.30–6pm; Nov–Feb Mon– Sat 9am–5pm, Sun 9–10.30am & 12.30– 2.30pm. Admission charge.

St Patrick's Cathedral was extensively restored in the 1860s

Spire

O'Connell Street's most dramatic sculptural addition in recent times is a steel spike, erected in 2002 (*see p46*). *O'Connell St.*

Temple Bar

Temple Bar, one of the oldest parts of Dublin, thrived on merchant ships and their traders during Viking and medieval times, but declined when the port was relocated to the eastern docks. In the 1990s the area was pedestrianised and developed into a cultural centre with the Gallery of Photography, Irish Film Centre and the Project Arts Centre located here. Arts and cultural events take place here year-round, but Temple Bar is most famous for its lively nightlife and is filled with cafés, restaurants, bars and nightclubs. *Temple Bar extends from Fishamble St just down from Christchurch in the west to Fleet St in the east, and from Dame St down to the river. Information service tel: (01) 677 2255. www.templebar.ie*

Trinity College

See pp42–3.

Waterways Visitor Centre

This informative centre uses audiovisual facilities and exhibitions to interpret the historical role of Ireland's inland waterways.

Grand Canal Basin, Ringsend, Dublin 2. Tel: (01) 677 7510. www.waterways ireland.org. Open: Wed–Sun 10am–6pm. Admission charge.

Trinity College

One of Dublin's three universities, Trinity is situated in busy College Green in the heart of the city. It was built on the site of an Augustinian Priory, All Hallows. Through the great arched gate, with its statues of two famous graduates, Oliver Goldsmith and Edmund Burke, is a spacious area of lawns and cobbled squares and gardens surrounded by buildings of various architectural styles and periods. The oldest part of the college is the Rubrics, a row of red-brick buildings dating from 1700.

Queen Elizabeth I founded Trinity College, the sole college of Dublin University, in 1592 as a seat of learning and the establishment of 'true religion' within the realm. Protestantism was the Queen's religion, and for centuries Catholics were prohibited from Trinity.

Today, Trinity College caters for around 8,000 students, following in the footsteps of such illustrious literary figures as Jonathan Swift, Samuel Beckett, Oscar Wilde and Bram Stoker. The novelist William Trevor, poets W J McCormack and Derek Mahon are more recent alumni. Women students have been admitted since 1903.

The tall campanile near the centre of Library Square was erected in 1853. Beyond it, screened by gracious maple trees and old lamps, is the famous library which houses many ancient volumes in the Long Room, including the famous *Book of Kells*.

The Long Room itself warrants inspection, with its barrel-vaulted ceiling 12.2m (40ft) high and tall shelves of leather-bound books, many of them accessible only by narrow

Historic Trinity College

Sculpture outside Trinity's library

ladder (but not by the public). Trinity has two-and-a-half-million books.

To the right of the entrance to the college is the Examination Hall, a former theatre. Its massive blackened doors must have struck terror into the heart of many a candidate. The hall is sometimes used for concerts. Like the Chapel opposite, which is shared by all Christian denominations, it has a barrel-vaulted ceiling and notable plasterwork. Near the Chapel is the college Dining Hall, which sometimes doubles as an examination room. *College Green, Dublin 2. Grounds open: daily 8am–10pm. Freely accessible; admission charge to view*

Book of Kells. Tel: (01) 896 2320. www.tcd.ie/Library/bookofkells. Library open: May–Sept Mon–Sat 9.30am–5pm, Sun 9.30am–4.30pm; Oct–Apr Mon–Sat 9.30–5pm, Sun noon–4.30pm. Admission charge.

BOOK OF KELLS

The *Book of Kells* is a richly coloured, minutely detailed version of the Gospels, written in Latin on vellum. Originally one volume, the vast book, regarded as one of the world's finest illuminated manuscripts, was divided into four when repairs were carried out in the 1950s. Two of these, opened at intricately decorated pages, can be closely examined by visitors (but be prepared for crowds) in the 'Book of Kells: Turning Darkness into Light' major exhibition.

Walk: Dublin's Old Town

This area has witnessed the Dublin story from its very beginnings. The Vikings arrived here in AD 841. Some 300 years later, Strongbow stormed the settlement, and a castle was built.

Allow 1½ hours.

Begin on Wellington Quay with Ha'penny Bridge behind you and head south.

1 Temple Bar area

This maze of narrow streets has developed into a trendy area of restaurants, cafés and bars, all tucked into the ageing warehouses formerly occupied by merchants and craftsmen.
Go west along Temple Bar, then left into Temple Lane and right into Dame St.

2 Dame Street

Dame Street's name derives from a dam once built on the River Poddle, now running underground. Here also, on the right, is Dublin's oldest surviving theatre, the Olympia.
Turn left into Castle St. Ahead is the gate to Upper Castle Yard.

3 Dublin Castle

Work on the castle began in 1205, although there are indications that defensive earthworks existed before the Vikings arrived. Guided tours of the castle and State Apartments are on offer (*see p30*). Also at the castle is the Chester Beatty Library (*see p29*).

Leave by the Justice Gate. Continue left along Castle St; turn left into Werburgh St/Bride St. Turn right into Kevin St Upper, then right into St Patrick's Close.

4 St Patrick's Cathedral

St Patrick's Cathedral dates from 1191. A bust of Jonathan Swift is at the west end of the nave (*see p41*). Nearby is Marsh's Library.
Turn right into Patrick St, left into Back Lane, and right into High St.

5 High Street

The Tailor's Hall in Back Lane, built around 1706, is Dublin's last surviving Guild Hall. The 'Back Lane Parliament' met here in 1792. Nearby, at St Audoen's Catholic Church (*see p40*), an audiovisual presentation tells the story of life in pre-Viking Ireland.
Cross Nicholas St/Winetavern St.

6 Christchurch Place

Built in the mid-11th century and re-built in stone by the Anglo-

Normans, Christ Church Cathedral contains the tomb of Strongbow, the Earl of Pembroke (*see pp29–30*).
Bear left along Christchurch Place to Fishamble St.

7 Fishamble Street

This was the birthplace of Archbishop Ussher, the poet James Clarence Mangan and the nationalist Henry Grattan, and witnessed the first ever performance of Handel's *Messiah*.
At the river turn right into Essex Quay.

8 Essex Quay

At the western end of Essex Quay, the Franciscan church of Saints Michael and John incorporates the remains of the Smock-Alley Theatre, built in 1661 and closed in the 1790s when the gallery collapsed. At the eastern end, Sunlight Chambers, built around 1900, has a terracotta frieze illustrating the manufacture and uses of soap.
Cross Parliament St and continue along Wellington Quay to end the walk back at Ha'penny Bridge.

Walk: Dublin's Old Town

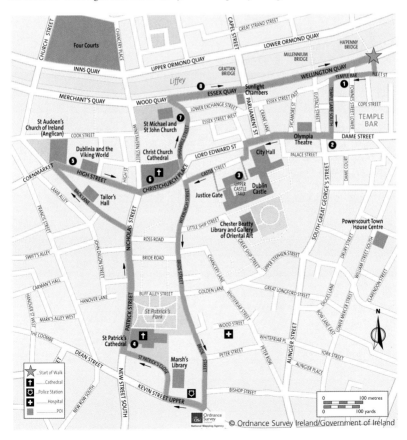

Walk: Dublin's cultural heart

North of the Liffey is Dublin's cultural heart. Here are the widest and largest streets, the best Georgian houses and the most splendid public buildings. Here also are the Abbey and Gate Theatres.

Allow 2 hours.

Begin on the north side of O'Connell Bridge, following Eden Quay to Custom House Quay.

1 Custom House

Dublin's most magnificent building. Since its opening in 1792, it has survived three major fires – the last, in 1921, was so fierce that brass fittings melted (*see p30*).
Return to Butt Bridge, turn right into Beresford Place, then left into Abbey St.

2 Abbey Street

The Abbey and Peacock Theatres were founded in 1904 by a group led by W B Yeats (*see p28*).
Turn right into O'Connell St.

3 O'Connell Street

O'Connell Street is one of the world's great thoroughfares. It is dominated by the Georgian majesty of the General Post Office, which was shelled and set ablaze when it became headquarters of the Irish Volunteers in the Easter Rising of 1916 (*see p32*).

In 2002, on the site of the old Nelson's Column, the Monument of Light was put up – a 120m (394ft) stainless-steel spire (*see p40*). Ambitious redevelopment plans are in progress for O'Connell Street.
Cross Parnell St to Parnell Square East.

4 Parnell Square

Originally known as the Barley Fields, Parnell Square dates from 1748 when it was laid out as pleasure gardens. On the left, beyond the monument to Charles Stewart Parnell, is the Gate Theatre, built in 1786 and converted to a theatre in 1930. Parnell Square North houses the Dublin Writers' Museum (*see pp31–2*) and the Hugh Lane Gallery (*see p33*).
Turn right into Granby Row.

5 Granby Row

Granby Row was the work of the Georgian developer Luke Gardiner, who had a profound influence throughout the city.
Turn left into Dorset St. Continue along Bolton St and turn right into Henrietta St.

6 Henrietta Street

Another Gardiner development, this was once the most fashionable street in Dublin. Now it is fairly run down.

At the end of Henrietta St pass through the central arch of King's Inns and cross the park to Constitution Hill. Turning left, continue to Church St. Turn right into May Lane.

7 The Old Jameson Distillery

Visitors get the chance to taste some different blends of Irish whiskey in this museum, found in what was The Old Jameson Distillery (*see p37*).

Turn left on to Bow St and then left again along Hammond Lane to Church St.

8 St Michan's Church

St Michan's contains a magnificent organ on which Handel is believed to have played. It also has a Penitent's Stool and a 16th-century chalice. But the church is best known for its limestone vaults where mummified bodies are on view (*see p40*). *Head south along Church St, turning left on to Inns Quay.*

9 Four Courts

The massive Georgian edifice confronting the Liffey is the seat of the Irish Law Courts. Columns of the portico still bear battle scars inflicted in 1922 during the civil war (*see p32*). *Continue parallel to the Liffey along Ormond Quay and complete the walk back to O'Connell Bridge.*

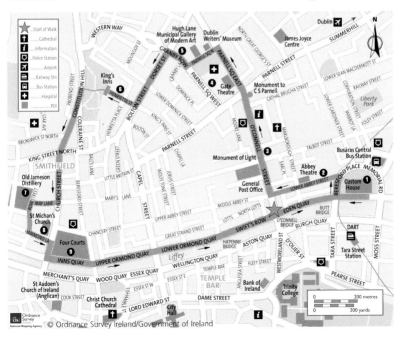

© Ordnance Survey Ireland/Government of Ireland

Casino Marino

Co Dublin

Several enjoyable attractions in County Dublin are dotted north and south along the coast and make a pleasant day out from the city. Historic castles, colourful gardens, stately homes, a 16th-century mill, a transport museum and a Martello tower where James Joyce once lived are easily reached by DART train from the city centre.

Casino Marino

Just north of Dublin, this 18th-century former summerhouse – not a casino in the gambling sense – is in the Palladian style. Pillars, stone lions and balustrades provide generous ornamentation, while inside there are elaborate plaster ceilings. Built for the 1st Earl of Charlemont, the Casino was restored in the early 1980s.
Malahide Rd, Marino. Tel: (01) 833 1618. Open: late Apr–late Oct daily 10am–5pm. Admission charge.

Drimnagh Castle

Drimnagh is the only Irish castle retaining a flooded moat, complete with waterfowl. It has a restored great hall, a battlement tower with lookout posts, a coach house, a folly tower and gardens laid out in formal 17th-century style.
Longanile Rd, Dublin 12. Tel: (01) 450 2530. Open: times vary, call to confirm. Admission charge.

Fernhill Gardens

These 100-hectare (247-acre) privately owned gardens are renowned for their camellias, rhododendrons, magnolias and azaleas. There is also a fine collection of trees more than 200 years old, a wild-flower meadow and a Victorian kitchen garden.
Sandyford. Tel: (0) 87 264 6053. Open: Tue–Sat 11am–5pm, Sun 2–5pm. Admission charge.

Howth Castle Gardens

The gardens, adjoining the Deer Park Hotel and Golf Courses, are best visited in May and early June. Started in 1854, they are famous for their rhododendrons – several thousands of them. Within the estate are the ruins of 16th-century Corr Castle and a Neolithic dolmen known as Aideen's Grave. The oldest part of Howth Castle dates from 1464, but it has been altered in every century since. The castle is closed to the public, but admission to the gardens is free.
Howth Castle, Howth. Tel: (01) 832

2624. *Open: daily 8am–dusk.*
Free admission.

Howth National Transport Museum

This small museum exhibits early fire engines, trucks, tractors and other vehicles. The Hill of Howth No. 9 train and a Giant's Causeway tram are among the stars of the show.
Howth Castle Demesne, Howth.
Tel: (01) 832 0427. www.national
transportmuseum.org. Open: Sat,
Sun & public holidays 2–5pm.
Admission charge.

James Joyce Museum

The Martello tower where Joyce spent a few weeks in 1904 as a guest of Oliver St John Gogarty is featured in his novel *Ulysses*, with Gogarty as the character of Buck Mulligan. Built in 1804, the tower contains a selection of Joyce memorabilia – the piano and guitar he played, a cigar case, a cane, manuscripts and a death mask of the author cast on 13 January 1941.
Sandycove. Tel: (01) 280 9265.
Open: Apr–Aug Tue–Sat 10am–1pm
& 2–5pm, Sun & public holidays 2–6pm
(closed Sun in Jun); winter by
appointment. Admission charge.

Malahide Castle

Except for a brief period when Cromwell evicted them, the Talbot family lived here continuously from 1185 to 1973, when the last Lord Talbot died. The Great Hall, which has a minstrels' gallery, contains many portraits, while the Oak Room and two drawing rooms contain 17th-, 18th- and 19th-century furniture. The castle has an antiques shop and there are picnic areas in the grounds.
Malahide. Tel: (01) 846 2184.
www.malahidecastle.com. Open:
Apr–Sept daily 10am–5pm; Oct–Mar
Sun & public holidays 11am–5pm.
Admission charge.

National Maritime Museum of Ireland

Housed in the 1837 Mariners' Church, this museum has, among many exhibits, an 11m (36ft) French longboat captured in Bantry Bay in 1796, and a noted collection of model ships on display.
Haigh Terrace, Dun Laoghaire.
Tel: (01) 280 0969. www.mariner.ie.
Open: from Easter 2012, call for opening
times. Admission charge.

Newbridge House

This Georgian house, built in 1737 for the Cobbe family, is now owned by Dublin County Council. A wealth of paintings hangs in the drawing room, and cabinets display many antique curiosities brought back by the Cobbe family from their world travels. The cobbled square has been restored and opened as a farm and museum of 18th-century rural life. There is also an aviary and a doll museum.
Donabate. Tel: (01) 843 6534.
www.fingalcoco.ie. Open: Apr–Sept

*Mon–Sat 10am–5pm, Sun & public
holidays noon–6pm; Oct–Mar Tue–Sun
& public holidays 11am–4pm.
Admission charge.*

Skerries Mills

Just outside the attractive fishing town
of Skerries, this 16th-century mill
contains a watermill and two
windmills. In the 1840s it was the
site of a bakery.
*Skerries. Tel: (01) 849 5208.
www.skerriesmills.org. Open: Apr–Sept
daily 10.30am–5.30pm; Oct–Mar daily
10.30am–4.30pm. Admission charge.*

Co Louth

Bordering Northern Ireland on one
side and the sea on another, Louth is
the smallest county in the Republic. It
contains several religious and historic
sites, as well as two of the country's
largest towns, Dundalk and Drogheda.

Battle of the Boyne Site

Forced to flee England because of
increasing opposition to his pro-

Catholic policies, King James II of
England landed in Ireland in 1689.
Here, he successfully raised an army
to try to re-establish himself, but
was defeated by his son-in-law, the
Protestant Prince William of Orange
(later William III), at the Battle of the
Boyne. The battle site, at the county
borders of Louth and Meath, is marked
by a large orange and green sign. The
campsites and the point where the river
was crossed are also marked. A trail
leaflet is available at the site.
*7km (4 miles) west of Drogheda.
Freely accessible.*

Millmount Museum

Contained in the buildings of an 18th-
century military barracks are relics
from Drogheda's trade, manufacturing
and domestic past. One interesting
exhibit is a leather-covered circular
coracle (small boat). This museum is
dramatically located above the town
on a hill.
*Millmount, Drogheda. Tel: (041) 983
3097. www.millmount.net. Open: Mon–*

The 12th-century Malahide Castle

Fishing boats at Skerries Harbour

Sat 9.30am–5pm, Sun & public holidays 2–5pm. Admission charge.

Old Mellifont Abbey

Little remains of Ireland's first Cistercian monastery, founded in 1142, though a substantial square gatehouse still stands, along with the ruins of a cloister, a two-storey octagonal lavabo and a 13th-century chapterhouse.
Tullyvallen, 10km (6 miles) west of Drogheda (signposted). Tel: (041) 982 6459. Open: late Apr–late Sept daily 10am–6pm. Last admission 5.15pm. Admission charge.

Proleek Dolmen

This 5,000-year-old mushroom-like stone structure has a capstone weighing over 46 tonnes. Nearby is a Bronze Age, wedge-shaped gallery grave.
Ballymascanlon, north of Dundalk. Freely accessible.

Co Meath

The rolling hills of County Meath were once home to the High Kings of Ireland. Today it is a repository for some of the country's most important Neolithic monuments and historic sites.

Boyne Valley/Newgrange Archaeological Site

The area known as Brú na Bóinne encompasses over 40 monuments, ranging from the massive megalithic tombs of Newgrange, Knowth and Dowth to a variety of standing stones and earthworks. Newgrange is one of Europe's most important Stone Age sites. The Newgrange passage grave, over 4,000 years old, predates the Pyramids of Egypt and is an extraordinary sight. The mound over the tomb, constructed with water-rolled pebbles, rises to a height of 11m (36ft) and is surrounded by an incomplete circle of stones. The passage is lined with huge stones, and mysterious 'artwork' in the form of geometrical symbols and spirals can be seen inside. A roof box incorporated in the structure allows the rays of the rising sun to penetrate a narrow slit and engulf the chamber with light – just briefly, once a year at the winter solstice. This phenomenon is reproduced artificially for the benefit of visitors. The Brú na Bóinne Visitor Centre interprets the archaeological heritage of the area and is the starting point for visits by bus to Newgrange and Knowth. Dowth is closed to the public.

Visitor centre: Donore, 11km (7 miles) southwest of Drogheda. Tel: (041) 988 0300. www.heritageireland.ie. Open: Feb–Apr & Oct daily 9.30am–5.30pm; May & mid-Sept–end Sept daily 9am–6.30pm; Jun–mid-Sept daily 9am–7pm; Nov–Jan daily 9am–5pm. Admission charge.

Hill of Tara

Famous as the seat of the High Kings of Ireland and an important site since the Stone Age, when a passage tomb was built, this was a major political and religious centre in pre-Christian times. Commanding majestic views over the fertile plains of Meath, it was abandoned in AD 1022 and now consists of grass-covered mounds, banks, wide ditches and earthworks. Displays in the interpretive centre help explain the site and its history, and its important features are more easily seen on a guided tour.

Tara, 13km (8 miles) south of Navan. Tel: (046) 902 5903. www.heritage ireland.ie. Interpretive centre open: late

A megalith stands guard at the Boyne Valley Archaeological Site

May–mid-Sept. Free admission; charge for interpretive centre.

Kells

The home of the *Book of Kells* in Trinity College Dublin (*see p43*). Little remains of the monastery – a few Celtic crosses and the ruins of the round tower.
Kells, 16km (10 miles) northwest of Navan.

Slane Hill

It was here in 433, tradition has it, that St Patrick proclaimed the arrival of Christianity and lit a paschal fire as a challenge to the High King of Tara. The hill provides a splendid view of the Boyne Valley.
13km (8 miles) west of Drogheda.

Trim Castle

Founded in 1173 by the Norman knight Hugh de Lacy, this is one of the largest intact medieval castles in Europe. It is often used as a film set and featured prominently in *Braveheart* (Mel Gibson, 1995). Cross the river to get a great view of the castle reflected in the Boyne.
Trim, 12km (7½ miles) south of Navan. Tel: (046) 943 8619. Open: Feb–Easter Sat & Sun 9.30am–5.30pm; Easter–Sept daily 10am–6pm; Oct daily 9.30am– 5.30pm; Nov–Jan Sat & Sun 9am–5pm. Admission charge.

Co Westmeath
Athlone Castle

The Anglo-Norman castle was a military post from its erection in the 13th century until 1969, when it was declared a National Monument. The visitor centre has a museum and audiovisual display. There is a folk and military museum in the keep, with relics of the town and district's history. The ground-floor section features local history and two early Sheela-na-gig sculptures.
St Peter's Square, Athlone. Tel: (090) 644 2100. www.athlone.ie. Open: from spring 2012, call for opening times. Admission charge.

Locke's Distillery Museum

Founded in 1757 and operational until 1953, this distillery, on the River Brosna, has been restored as an industrial museum and craft enterprise centre.
Dublin–Galway road (N6), Kilbeggan. Tel: (057) 933 2134. www.lockes distillerymuseum.ie. Open: (tour & whiskey tasting) Apr–Oct daily 9am– 6pm; Nov–Mar daily 10am–4pm. Admission charge.

Co Longford
Corlea Trackway Visitor Centre

The visitor centre houses part of a bog road built from oak beams in 140 BC, preserved by the acid nature of the boglands. Most of the road remains beneath the bog.
Corlea Trackway Centre, Keenagh. Tel: (043) 332 2386. www. heritageireland.ie. Open: early Apr– Sept daily 10am–6pm. Free admission.

Round towers and castles

Ireland's is a landscape of fantasy. Every scene, it seems – on mountainside, riverbank or rocky shore – bears an exclamation mark of history in the form of a round tower or ruined castle.

Close your eyes and it is not difficult to conjure up figures from the past: hooded monks sprinting across the turf and pulling up the ladders against another gang of Viking raiders; minstrels making music while the lords and ladies feast; silhouettes flitting among flames as dark deeds are committed.

Round towers

The 70 or so pencil-shaped round towers – unique to Ireland – which survive throughout the country date mainly from the 9th century. Built near ecclesiastical sites, especially monasteries, they served as bell towers, storehouses and watchtowers.

Varying in height from 15 to 45m (49 to 148ft), and usually tapering towards a stone cone-shaped top, the towers had a door set high enough above the ground to require a ladder for entry. This could be hauled in during an attack. Most towers originally had a number of floors reached by ladders and trapdoors, but some, probably used only as

Kildare Cathedral's 10th-century round tower

Kilkenny Castle, a blend of Gothic and classical styles

watchtowers, had a stairway. Among the best-preserved towers are those at Ardmore, Co Waterford; Cashel, Co Tipperary; Cloyne, Co Cork; Devenish Island, Co Fermanagh; Glendalough, Co Wicklow; and Monasterboice, Co Louth.

Castles

The first stone castles – the earliest were timber constructions – were built by Norman colonists between 1190 and 1215. The grandest were those in Dublin, Kilkenny and Limerick.

Many of Ireland's castles date from a 15th-century building boom among such influential families as the MacCarthys (Blarney, Co Cork), the MacConmaras (Bunratty, Co Clare) and the MacNamaras (Knappogue, Co Clare). Bunratty and Knappogue are best known now for hosting medieval banquets.

Co Offaly
Birr Castle Demesne

Home of the Earls of Rosse, the castle is not open to the public, but the beautiful 40-hectare (99-acre) gardens are. Plants from remote parts of the world grow in these gardens, famous for the world's highest box hedge (10m/32ft), and for the permanent exhibition of the Rosse telescope, the world's largest when it was built in the mid-19th century.

Birr. Tel: (057) 912 0336. www.birrcastle. com. Open: mid-Mar–Oct daily 9am–6pm; Nov–mid-Mar daily 10am–4pm. Admission charge.

Clonmacnoise

One of Ireland's most sacred sites and former burial place of the kings of Connacht and Tara, this monastic settlement, founded by St Ciarán in AD 545, contains two round towers, the remains of a cathedral, nine church ruins, three high crosses, a 13th-century castle and over 200 grave slabs. The Nuns' Chapel and the 10th-century Cross of the Scriptures are particularly noted for the quality of the mason's craft.

Shannonbridge. Tel: (090) 967 4195. Open: mid-Mar–May & Sept–Oct daily 10am–6pm; Jun–Aug daily 9am–7pm; Nov–mid-Mar daily 10am–5.30pm. Admission charge.

Tullamore Dew Heritage Centre

Irish Mist connoisseurs will love this place – after the visit to the restored bonded warehouse, you get a

Birr Castle, an impressive fortified manor house set in extensive grounds

complimentary taste. The distillery once dominated the town and the heritage centre details the lives of the people and their relations with the company that employed them.

Bury Quay, Tullamore. Tel: (057) 932 5015. www.tullamore-dew.org. Open: May–Sept Mon–Sat 9am–6pm, Sun noon–5pm; Oct–Apr Mon–Sat 10am–5pm, Sun noon–5pm.

Co Kildare
Castletown House

Ireland's first, and most important, Palladian mansion was built in the 1720s for William Conolly, Speaker of the Irish Parliament. Its elegant interior includes fine examples of 18th-century furniture and superb plasterwork by the Francini brothers.

Celbridge. Tel: (01) 628 8252. www. castletownhouse.ie. Open: Apr–Oct Tue–Sun 10am–4.45pm. Guided tours only. Admission charge.

Irish National Stud and Japanese Gardens

Tour the National Stud, where many of Ireland's famous thoroughbred

racehorses have been bred and nurtured, and its Horse Museum. Then visit the adjoining Japanese Gardens, established in 1906 and thought by many to be the finest in Europe. Their design symbolises the life cycle of Man.
Tully, 1.5km (1 mile) south of Kildare town. Tel: (045) 522963/521617. www.irish-national-stud.ie. Open: mid-Feb–Oct daily 9.30am–6pm; Nov daily 9.30am–5pm. Tours: Feb–Oct daily noon, 2.30pm & 4pm; Nov daily 1pm. Admission charge.

Straffan Steam Museum
This model railway collection depicts the development of the Irish locomotive since the 18th century. Also on display are full-size stationary steam engines.
Lodge Park, Straffan. Tel: (01) 627 3155. www.steam-museum.com. Open: Jun–Aug Wed–Sun & public holidays 2–6pm. Admission charge.

Co Laois
Emo Court and Gardens
A fine Georgian mansion designed by James Gandon. Its great rotunda is lit by a lantern in the dome. The gardens

The Japanese Gardens, laid out by Japanese gardener Eida and his son Minoru

contain fine statuary, an imposing lake and avenues of yews.
Emo. Tel: (057) 862 6573. House open: Easter–end Sept daily 10am–6pm. Guided tours only. Gardens open: daily dawn–dusk. Admission charge to house; free admission to gardens.

Rock of Dunamase
The remains of a Norman castle are dramatically perched on a limestone hill. Great views of surrounding countryside from the top.
Off the N80 between Portlaoise & Stradbally.

Stradbally Steam Museum
A collection of steam machinery, from a Guinness® Loco Engine used on the streets of the brewery to a home-made steam tractor.
Irish Steam Preservation Society, The Green, Stradbally. Tel: (057) 864 1878. www.irishsteam.ie. Open: for rallies & public holidays. Admission charge.

Windy Gap
The Carlow to Stradbally road (N8) passes through Windy Gap, one of Ireland's most famous scenic drives. Stop at the Windy Gap car park for a long look over the Barrow Valley, with its wide vistas of the surrounding countryside.

Co Carlow
Altamont Gardens
Known as the most romantic in Ireland, these fine gardens were first planted in

1850 and are still being added to.
*Off the N80 & N81, Tullow. Tel: (059)
915 9444. www.heritageireland.ie. Open:
Easter–Sept daily 9am–6.30pm; Oct
daily 9am–5pm; Nov–Easter Mon–Thur
9am–4.30pm, Fri 9am–3.30pm. Free
admission; charge for guided tour.*

Browne's Hill Dolmen
This impressive dolmen, which dates
from around 2500 BC, has the largest
capstone in Ireland, and may even be the
largest in Europe, estimated to weigh
more than 101 tonnes. Its front end still
stands, while the rear has collapsed and
rests on the ground.
*Hacketstown Rd, R726, Carlow.
Freely accessible (a path leads from the
parking area).*

Carlow Castle
Carlow's ruined 13th-century castle
has witnessed much bloodshed
throughout its turbulent history. The
castle survived attack from Cromwell's
forces in the 17th century, but was
badly damaged 150 years later during
attempts to reduce the thickness of the
walls by using explosives. These ancient
fortifications are on the east bank of
the River Barrow in Carlow.
Freely accessible.

Co Wicklow
Dotted with stately homes and lush
estate grounds, County Wicklow is
known as the Garden of Ireland. From
the pretty green vales to the rugged
Wicklow Mountains, it provides a

Ruins at Avoca

wealth of scenic beauty on Dublin's
doorstep.

Avoca
The village of Avoca is set in its
picturesque valley, where the
confluence of two rivers, the Avonbeg
and the Avonmore, inspired Thomas
Moore to write his famous poem *The
Meeting of the Waters* in 1807. The
oldest hand-weaving mill in Ireland,
Avoca Handweavers, still produces
textiles in the traditional way and
welcomes visitors.
*4km (2½ miles) south of Avondale.
Avoca Handweavers: tel: (0402) 35105.
Open: daily 9am–6pm; winter daily
9.30am–5.30pm. Free admission.*

Avondale House
Avondale is the restored home of the
nationalist leader Charles Stewart
Parnell (1846–91). Part of the house
is devoted to a museum.
*Rathdrum. Tel: (0404) 46111. www.
coillte.ie. Open: Jul & Aug daily 11am–*

*6pm; Sept & Oct Tue–Sun 11am–6pm.
Admission charge.*

Glendalough

Glendalough is the setting of Ireland's
most important early Christian
settlement, founded by St Kevin in the
6th century. It grew into a centre of
learning and its fame spread throughout
Europe. Visitors to the ancient ruin site
can see a near-perfect round tower, a
church with fine Irish Romanesque
decoration, an oratory (St Kevin's
Kitchen) and a 10th-century cathedral.
A **visitor centre** houses an exhibition
and audiovisual show. There is some
great day hillwalking from Glendalough.
*16km (10 miles) west of Wicklow.
Visitor centre: tel: (0404) 45325.
www.heritageireland.ie. Open: mid-
Mar–mid-Oct daily 9.30am–6pm (last
admission 5.15pm); mid-Oct–mid-Mar
daily 9.30am–5pm. Admission charge for
visitor centre.*

Mount Usher Gardens

Mount Usher is one of the finest
examples of a 'wild garden', planted

The church at Glendalough

along the banks of the River Vartry. Laid
out in 1868, it contains rare trees, shrubs
and flowers from all over the world,
including 70 species of eucalyptus.
*On the main Dublin–Rosslare road,
Ashford. Tel: (0404) 40116. www.mount
ushergardens.ie. Open: late Feb–Oct
daily 10.30am–6pm. Admission charge.*

Powerscourt Gardens

The main block of this Palladian-style
house was gutted by fire in 1974, but an
exhibition of photographs shows its
former glory. The gardens, however, are
magnificent. Containing English, Italian
and Japanese sections, they are rich in
sculptures, and include a fountain, lake,
terraces, formal flower beds and
conifers. Some 5km (3 miles) away is
spectacular **Powerscourt Waterfall**, at
120m (394ft) the highest in Ireland.
*Enniskerry, near Bray. Tel: (01) 204
6000. www.powerscourt.ie. Open: daily
9.30am–5.30pm; winter daily until dusk.
Separate admission charges for
exhibition, gardens & waterfall.*

Russborough House

This mid-18th-century mansion with
its sumptuous plasterwork is home to
the Beit Collection of paintings, which
includes works by Gainsborough,
Murillo and Velázquez. Two infamous
robberies took place here: one in 1974
when the IRA stole £8 million in
artworks, and the second in 1986
when larger-than-life criminal Michael
Cahill drove away with paintings worth
£30 million.

Blessington. Tel: (045) 865239. www. russborough.ie. Open: Apr & Oct Sun & public holidays 10am–6pm; May–Sept daily 10am–6pm. Admission charge.

Co Kilkenny
Dunmore Cave

The human bones and coins that have been found in this natural limestone cavern suggest that Vikings may have caused many deaths here in 928.

Well-lit walkways lead through the cave, illuminating enormous stalagmite and stalactite formations, and a small centre explains the history and geology.
Off the N78, Ballyfoyle, 11km (7 miles) north of Kilkenny. Tel: (056) 776 7726. www.heritageireland.ie. Open: Mar–mid-Jun & mid-Sept–Oct daily 9.30am–5pm; mid-Jun–mid-Sept daily 9.30am–6.30pm; Nov–Mar Wed–Sun 9.30am–5pm. Guided tours only. Admission charge.

Jerpoint Abbey

This 12th-century Cistercian abbey is one of Ireland's finest ruins, with detailed carvings in the cloisters.
On the N9, 3.5km (2 miles) south of Thomastown. Tel: (056) 772 4623. www.heritageireland.ie. Open: early Mar–Sept daily 9am–5.30pm; Oct daily 9am–5pm; Nov daily 9.30am–4pm. Last admission 45 mins before closing. Admission charge.

Kilkenny Castle

Set above the waters of the River Nore, imposing 12th-century Kilkenny Castle, remodelled in Victorian times, is noted for its restored great hall and extensive art gallery. The Butler Gallery houses exhibitions of modern art. Visit the nearby Kilkenny Design Centre to see the best in Irish craftwork.
The Parade, Kilkenny. Tel: (056) 770 4100. www.kilkennycastle.ie. Open: Mar daily 9.30am–5pm; Apr, May & Sept daily 9.30am–5.30pm; Jun–Aug daily 9am–5.30pm; Oct–Feb daily 9.30am–4.30pm. Guided tours only. Admission charge; free admission to grounds.

Rothe House

A charming example of a 16th-century town house with a fine art collection and exhibition of period costumes.
Parliament St, Kilkenny. Tel: (056) 772 2893. www.rothehouse.com. Open: Apr–Oct Mon–Sat 10.30am–5pm, Sun 3–5pm; Nov–Mar Mon–Sat 10.30am–4.30pm. Admission charge.

St Canice's Cathedral

Renowned for its grandeur, carvings and marble monuments, St Canice's Cathedral was built in the 13th century.

After its dissolution in 1540, Jerpoint Abbey was granted to the Ormonde family

The nearby 9th-century round tower can be climbed, weather permitting.
Kilkenny. Tel: (056) 776 4971. www.stcanicescathedral.com. Open: Apr, May & Sept Mon–Sat 10am–1pm & 2–5pm, Sun 2–5pm; Jun–Aug Mon–Sat 9am–6pm, Sun 1–6pm; Oct–Mar Mon–Sat 10am–1pm & 2–4pm, Sun 2–4pm. Admission charge.

Kilkenny Castle

Co Wexford
Dunbrody Famine Ship
A replica of one of the emigrant ships that took the Irish in their droves to America. The great-grandparents of JFK left from this spot in New Ross.
South Quay, New Ross. Tel: (051) 425239. www.dunbrody.com. Open: Apr–Sept daily 9am–6pm; Oct–Mar daily 9am–5pm. Admission charge.

Hook Lighthouse Visitor Centre
An 800-year-old tower that still carries out its function as a lighthouse. The visitor centre offers guided tours of the lighthouse and the view from the balcony is terrific.
Hook Lighthouse, Hook Head, Fethard-on-Sea. Tel: (051) 397054. www.hook heritage.ie. Open: May & Sept daily 9.30am–5.30pm; Jun–Aug daily 9.30am–6pm; Oct–Apr daily 9.30am–5pm. Admission charge.

Irish National Heritage Park
This open-air site is a good overview of Ireland, from prehistoric to medieval times. It includes authentic reconstructions of Stone Age and Bronze Age settlements and a Norman motte and bailey.
Ferrycarrig. Tel: (053) 912 0733. www.inhp.ie. Open: May–Aug daily 9.30am–6.30pm (last admission 5pm); Sept–Apr daily 9.30am–5.30pm. Times may be subject to seasonal change. Admission charge.

John F Kennedy Arboretum
This collection of 4,500 species of tree and shrub is set in 252 hectares (623 acres). In summer, visitors can tour it on foot, by pony and trap or miniature railway.
1km (7$^1/_2$ miles) south of New Ross. Tel: (051) 388171. www.heritageireland.ie. Open: Apr & Sept daily 10am–6.30pm; May–Aug daily 10am–8pm; Oct–Mar daily 10am–5pm. Admission charge.

Wexford Wildfowl Reserve
Bewick swans, white-fronted geese, pintails, gulls and other species winter on the mudflats of this wildlife reserve on the Slaney Estuary. It also has walks, an observation tower, hides, a visitor centre and wildfowl identification charts.
North Sloblands. Tel: (053) 912 3129. Open: daily 9am–5pm. Free admission.

Munster

Munster contains the counties of Tipperary, Waterford, Cork, Kerry, Limerick and Clare. Its terrain is as varied as Ireland itself, from the Golden Plain of Tipperary to the rugged coastlines of Cork, the mountains of Kerry and the majestic Cliffs of Moher in Clare. Here, the past and present merge. The ancient ring forts and dolmens and the mystic Rock of Cashel share the province with three of Ireland's largest industrial cities: Cork, Limerick and Waterford.

CO TIPPERARY

Tipperary is Ireland's largest inland county. It is ringed by mountains on the south and west, with the tranquil waters of Lough Derg lapping against its northern border. In between, the rich land of the Golden Vale fans out from the River Suir. Here you'll find some of the region's finest castles and historic sites.

Cahir Castle

Built on a rocky island in the middle of the River Suir, Cahir Castle, one of the best preserved in Ireland, has been impressively restored. Built in the 15th and 16th centuries, its oldest parts (an earlier structure) date from 1164. Furnishings are authentic reproductions of the period. Scenes for the films *Excalibur* and *Barry Lyndon* were shot here, and there are guided tours. An audiovisual presentation highlights the area's antiquities.
Cahir. Tel: (052) 744 1011.
www.heritageireland.ie. Open: mid-Mar–mid-Jun & Sept–mid-Oct daily 9.30am–5.30pm; mid-Jun–Aug daily 9am–6.30pm; mid-Oct–mid-Mar daily 9.30am–4.30pm. Admission charge.

Cashel
Bolton Library

A fine collection of illuminated manuscripts, books and maps. Exhibitions of printing, antique books and silver are frequently staged.
Grounds of St John the Baptist Cathedral, John St, Cashel.
Tel: (062) 61232. Open: Mon–Thur & Sat 10am–3pm. Admission charge.

Brú Ború Cultural Centre

Named after Brian Ború, the 11th-century High King of Ireland, this cultural village incorporates a folk theatre, craft centre, information centre and a computerised genealogy service. Music, drama and banquets are held from Tuesday to Saturday evenings throughout the summer, and the restaurant serves Irish fare.

Near the Rock of Cashel.
Tel: (062) 61122. www.bruboru.ie.
Open: mid-Jun–mid-Sept daily 9am–
11.30pm; rest of year Mon–Fri 9am–
5pm (Nov–Easter Fri until 2pm).
Jun–Sept evening performances.
Admission charge.

Cashel Folk Village

Cashel Folk Village is an interesting
collection of reconstructed houses and
shops displaying furniture, artefacts
and tools portraying local life from the
18th to the 20th centuries. The
butcher's shop would put you off meat.
Dominick St, Cashel. Tel: (062) 63601.
www.cashelfolkvillage.ie. Open: Jan–
mid-Mar & mid-Oct–mid-Dec daily
9.30am–4.30pm; mid-Mar–mid-Jun &

mid-Sept–mid-Oct daily 9.30am–
5.30pm; mid-Jun–mid-Sept daily
9am–7.30pm. Admission charge.

Cashel Heritage Centre

The story of the kings of Cashel from
AD 300 is featured in Cashel Heritage
Centre. Tram rides in summer.
Main St, Cashel. Tel: (062) 62511.
Open: Mar–Oct daily 9.30am–5.30pm;
Nov–Feb Mon–Fri 9.30am–5.30pm.
Free admission.

Rock of Cashel

The Rock of Cashel – the Gaelic word
means 'stone fort' – soars 60m (197ft)
above the Golden Vale. Legend has it that
the Devil took a bite out of the nearby
Slieve Bloom Mountains and spat it out

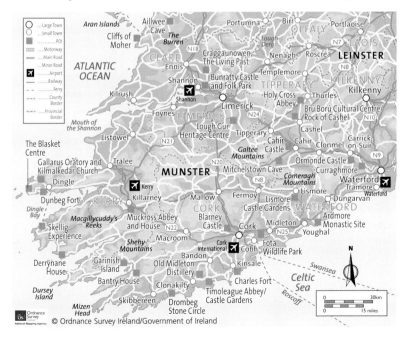

© Ordnance Survey Ireland/Government of Ireland

on to the plains when he was surprised by St Patrick.

Crowning the rock is a wealth of medieval architecture. The oldest building, the Round Tower, is thought to date from the 10th century, but it is certain that the site was hallowed in pre-Christian times. The High Kings of Munster are said to have been crowned on the summit.

Cormac's Chapel, completed in 1134, is the best preserved of the Rock's buildings and is also the earliest of Ireland's surviving Romanesque churches. It was built by Cormac MacCarthy, King of Desmond and Bishop of Cashel, and its twisted columns, steeply pitched roof and fine carvings contribute to its unique beauty.

St Patrick's Cathedral, the largest building, was built about a century later than the chapel. The 13th-century building was burnt down in 1495 and restored in the 16th century. The Apostles and scenes from the Apocalypse are represented in sculptures in the north transept, and there is a splendid view of the surrounding vale from the top of the central tower.

The Hall of Vicars is the first building to be reached by those approaching the Rock from Cashel town. It was built in the 15th century for eight vicars who assisted in the cathedral services. On the ground floor is the original St Patrick's Cross (the one outside is a replica), a high cross less ornately carved than usual.

Rock of Cashel, stronghold of the kings of Munster for over 700 years

Cashel. Tel: (062) 61437. www.heritage ireland.ie. Open: mid-Mar–early Jun & early Sept–mid Oct daily 9am–5.30pm; early Jun–early Sept daily 9am–7pm; mid-Oct–mid-Mar daily 9am–4.30pm. Last admission 45 mins before closing. Admission charge.

Holy Cross Abbey

Founded in 1180, left derelict for 400 years, and totally restored between 1971 and 1985, the abbey thrives as a parish church. It incorporates architecture of the 12th and 15th centuries, with excellent stone carvings and window traceries.
On the R660, 6km (4 miles) south of Thurles. Tel: (0504) 43124. www.holy crossabbey.ie. Open: daily 10.30am–6pm. Donations welcome.

Mitchelstown Cave

Visitors can take an escorted tour
through the spectacular rock formations
of these massive, high-ceilinged
chambers, only recently discovered.
*Burncourt, midway between Cahir &
Mitchelstown. Tel: (052) 746 7246.
www.mitchelstowncave.com. Open: daily
10am–5.30pm; Oct–Mar closing time
varies. Admission charge.*

Nenagh Heritage Centre

Nenagh's former county gaol houses
the town's heritage centre. It features
the excellent 'Lifestyles in Northwest
Tipperary' exhibition and there are
frequent temporary displays of
paintings and photographs.
*The Governor's House, Nenagh, opposite
the Castle Keep. Tel: (067) 33850. Open:
mid-May–Aug Mon–Fri 9.30am–5pm,
Sat 10am–5pm; Sept–mid-May Mon–Fri
9.30am–5pm. Free admission.*

Ormonde Castle

Ireland's best example of a fortified
Elizabethan manor house, Ormonde
Castle was built in the 1560s alongside
an older building overlooking the River
Suir. It is said to have been built by the
Earl of Ormonde to entertain Elizabeth
I, who never arrived. The older castle is
reputed to be the birthplace of Anne
Boleyn, wife of Henry VIII.
*Castle Park, Carrick-on-Suir. Tel: (051)
640787. www.heritageireland.ie. Open:
mid-Apr–early Oct daily 10am–6pm.
Guided tours only. Last admission
45 mins before closing. Admission charge.*

Tipperary County Museum

This quality county museum has wide-
ranging displays of 19th- and early
20th-century items of political, civic
and industrial interest, photography, art
and sports collections and more, which
are excellently presented. The museum
also features an ongoing programme of
visiting exhibitions.
*Emmett St, Clonmel. Tel: (052) 613 4550.
Open: Tue–Sat 10am–5pm. Free
admission.*

CO WATERFORD

The coast of County Waterford has
some of Ireland's most popular beach
resorts, as well as quaint fishing
villages, striking cliffs and, inland,
scenic rivers, mountains and castle
gardens. It is also home to one of
Ireland's oldest Christian sites, and
its first Viking settlement in
Waterford city.

Ardmore Monastic Site

According to legend, 30 years before
St Patrick arrived in Ireland in the 5th
century, St Declan crossed from Wales
and established a monastic settlement
at Ardmore. He chose a magnificent
location, affording stunning views over
the bay. The area surrounding the site is
known as Old Parish and is believed to
be the oldest parish in Ireland.

The site of the saint's original
monastic foundation is today marked
by an exceptionally well-preserved
11th-century round tower in the
ruined **Cathedral of St Declan**. The

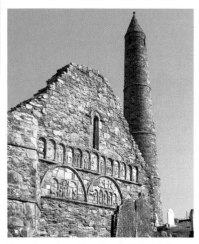

Carved murals on the old cathedral at Ardmore

surrounding graveyard, pitching steeply towards the coast, contains St Declan's Oratory, where the saint is believed to be buried. Though the years have taken their toll, and the old cathedral is now roofless, it is an evocative place, especially when one views the strikingly carved murals, the *Adoration of the Magi*, *Fall of Man*, *Judgement of Solomon* and the *Weighing of Souls*. *Signposted off the N25 between Dungarvan (Co Waterford) & Youghal (Co Cork). Freely accessible.*

Curraghmore

This house has been the ancestral home of Lord Waterford and his forebears since 1170. Detailed plasterwork is a feature of the interior.

The beautiful grounds surrounding Curraghmore contain a fine arboretum, an 18th-century shell grotto (designed and built by the Countess of Tyrone),

and a 13th-century bridge which spans the River Clogagh.
Portlaw. Tel: (051) 387101. www.curraghmorehouse.ie. Grounds & shell house open: Easter–mid-Oct Tue–Thur 10am–4pm & 1st & 3rd Sun of month. Tours of house, shell house & gardens. Admission charge.

Lismore
Lismore Castle Gardens

One of several places linked with Edmund Spenser's poem *The Faerie Queene*, the gardens have a fine collection of shrubs, including camellias and magnolias, and restful woodland walks. A dramatic yew walk is believed to be more than 800 years old.

The Irish home of the Dukes of Devonshire, the estate was once leased to Sir Walter Raleigh. The present castle was built in the mid-19th century, and a new gallery has recently been opened. *Signposted in Lismore. Tel: (058) 54424. Open: Mar–Sept daily 11am–4.45pm. Admission charge.*

Lismore Heritage Centre

Lismore has a rich history: founded as a monastic centre in AD 636, it became a famous seat of learning, was sacked repeatedly by Vikings and Normans, and became involved in many religious and political struggles. The story is told in an audiovisual presentation.
The Courthouse, Lismore. Tel: (058) 54975. www.discoverlismore.com.

Open: Mon–Fri 9.30am–5.30pm, Sat 10am–5pm, Sun noon–5pm. Admission charge. Walking tours leave from the heritage centre daily 11am & 3pm. Separate charge.

Waterford
Bishop's Palace
Waterford is known for its splendid 18th-century architecture, and the Bishop's Palace is one of its finest examples. Inside it tells the story of the city from 1700 to the 1970s, with displays of beautiful furniture, artworks, silver and glassware, including the world's oldest piece of Waterford crystal.
At the end of Waterford Mall. Tel: (051) 849650. www.waterfordtreasures.com. Open: Jun–Aug Mon–Sat 9am–6pm, Sun 11am–6pm; Sept–May Mon–Sat 10am–5pm, Sun 11am–5pm. Admission charge.

Christ Church Cathedral
Designed by John Roberts, a Waterford architect whose work included the city's Holy Trinity Cathedral, Christ Church is an ornate Renaissance-style structure built in the 1770s to replace a church which had stood on the site since the 11th century.

Standing in a pleasant square, the Church of Ireland cathedral contains interesting monuments, including the 15th-century tomb of James Rice, depicting a decaying corpse.

Across the square from the cathedral is the roofless **French Church**, founded as a Franciscan friary in 1240 and later used by Huguenot refugees. It has a fine east window and the tomb of Sir Neal O'Neill, who fled with James II after his defeat at the hands of William of Orange at the Battle of the Boyne.
Cathedral Square, Waterford. Tel: (051) 858958. www.christchurchwaterford.com. Open: Jun–Sept Mon–Fri 9am–6pm, Sat 10am–4pm; Oct Mon–Fri 10am–5pm, Sat 10am–4pm. Donations expected.

Holy Trinity Cathedral
The simple exterior of Waterford's Roman Catholic cathedral, also designed by John Roberts, conceals an extravagantly decorated interior hung with chandeliers of Waterford crystal.
Barronstrand St, Waterford. Tel: (051) 875166. www.waterford-cathedral.com. Freely accessible.

Lismore Castle

Reginald's Tower Museum

Originally built by the Vikings in 1003 as part of Waterford's defences, in its time it has served as a royal residence, a mint, a gaol and an arsenal. It now holds a splendid collection of Viking artefacts.

The Quay, Waterford. Tel: (051) 304220. Open: Easter–May daily 10am–5pm; Jun–mid-Sept daily 10am–6pm; mid-Sept–Easter Wed–Sun 10am–5pm. Admission charge.

Waterford City Hall

This fine Georgian building dates from 1783 and incorporates the Theatre Royal. A huge Waterford glass chandelier, made in 1802, hangs in the council chamber (a copy can be found in Philadelphia's Independence Hall).

The Mall, Waterford. Tel: (051) 873501. Open: Mon–Fri 10am–5pm. Free admission.

Blarney Castle

CO CORK

Ireland's largest county has it all, from its bustling capital, Cork City, to the stunning scenery on its rocky peninsulas jutting into the Atlantic. Attractions range from the ancient stone circles dotted through the countryside to stately homes, the famous Blarney Castle, and the foodie capital of Kinsale.

Bantry House

Exquisitely set in Italianate gardens overlooking the magnificent bay, this Georgian mansion dates from around 1740. There are extensive collections of art and antiques, including a tapestry made for Marie Antoinette. The French Armada Interpretive Centre, also located here, contains documents, weapons and artefacts from a ship which sank during the French invasion attempt of 1796. The house is also the perfect setting for classical music performances throughout the year.

Outskirts of Bantry. Tel: (027) 50047. www.bantryhouse.com. Open: Mar–Oct daily 10am–6pm. Admission charge.

Blarney Castle

Built around 1446, the castle was the stronghold of the MacCarthys, and it was Dermot MacCarthy, Lord Blarney, whose smooth talk and empty promises exasperated Elizabeth I and brought a new word into the English language. To acquire this 'gift of the gab' (eloquence), visitors must first climb over 120 steps, then lie on their back, hang over an open space and kiss the legendary Blarney Stone. The central keep, all that remains of the old castle, is set in pleasantly landscaped gardens and there are good views of the surrounding Lee Valley.

On the R617, 8km (5 miles) northwest of Cork. Tel: (021) 438 5252. www.blarney castle.ie. Open: May & Sept Mon–Sat 9am–6.30pm, Sun 9am–5.30pm; Jun–Aug Mon–Sat 9am–7pm, Sun 9am–5.30pm; Oct–Apr daily 9am–sunset. Admission charge.

Kinsale

Ireland's gourmet capital (*see box*).

Charles Fort

Built in the late 17th century after the defeat of the Spanish and Irish in the Battle of Kinsale, this is one of Europe's most complete star forts (so-called because of its shape). Covering some 5 hectares (12 acres) on a cliff-top site, it was occupied by British troops until 1920.

Glandore, Co Cork

Summer Cove, 3km (2 miles) east of Kinsale. Tel: (021) 477 2263. www.heritageireland.ie. Open: mid-Mar–Oct daily 10am–6pm; Nov–mid-Mar daily 10am–5pm. Admission charge.

Drombeg Stone Circle

The Cork–Kerry region has the highest concentration of stone circles in Ireland, and Drombeg Circle is one of the most accessible. It stands in a small field with a commanding sea view.

(*Cont. on p74*)

GOURMET CAPITAL

Kinsale hit on a grand idea over 30 years ago, which was to have a food festival just as the season was dying down a bit – called the International Gourmet Festival. It is held every October, and lasts for four days when the twelve participating restaurants put on special offers and festival-goers get to try out some new ideas and tastes in food.

Calling itself Ireland's gourmet capital may be a bit over the top when you consider some of the excellent restaurants in Dublin and Belfast, but the small village certainly has a claim to recognition for its cuisine and for some excellent places to eat all year round. Fishy Fishy's reputation just seems to grow as its premises expands, while Jim Edwards offers a relaxed modern Irish style in both food and ambience. The Blue Haven prides itself on seeking out locally caught fish and home-grown vegetables.

There are places to suit all budgets and tastes in Kinsale, plus it's a great place to shop for crafts, dabble your toes in the water and watch the yachts put in.

Walk: Cork City

Cork is built on an island embraced by two channels of the River Lee. The city's twisting, hilly streets and narrow lanes create traffic delays at times, so walking is the best way to get around. There is much to enjoy in a city which has retained some of the old ambience of a tall ship's port.

Allow 1½ hours. Opposite Opera House Bridge, then begin at St Patrick's Bridge. Proceed right along Lavitt's Quay. turn left into Emmet Place.

1 Emmet Place

The concrete drabness of Cork's Opera House may come as a disappointment, but the theatre offers a full programme of classical and popular opera, ballet and drama. The adjacent Crawford Municipal Art Gallery has an extensive collection of local landscapes from the 18th and 19th centuries. Temporary exhibitions are also staged.

At the bottom of Emmet Place continue west along Paul St.

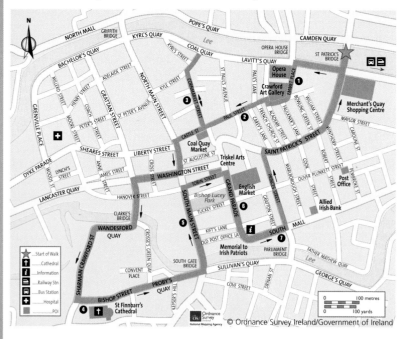

© Ordnance Survey Ireland/Government of Ireland

2 Paul Street

Pedestrianised Paul Street in the heart of the city centre has restaurants, art and craft studios and street entertainment in an attractive piazza. Traditional Irish goods are available in the shops.
Continue west to the junction of Cornmarket St and Castle St.

3 Cornmarket Street

Coal Quay Market stands at the junction where an open-air market once spread along the length of Cornmarket Street. Today, the bulk of the area's trade is in second-hand clothing and antiques.
Follow Castle St, turning left at North Main St and right into Washington St. At Grattan St turn left, cross Clarke's Bridge and turn right on to Wandesford Quay, following Sharman Crawford St to Bishop St.

4 St Finnbarr's Cathedral

The cathedral's three spires give it a medieval look, but the building dates from the 19th century. It stands on the site of a monastery founded by St Finbarr in 650 (*see p75*).
Follow Bishop St to Proby's Quay, re-crossing the river at South Gate Bridge.

5 South Main Street

South Main Street leads to two further centres of art and culture. Bishop Lucey Park, on the right, has a permanent exhibition of modern Cork sculpture. Also on the right, narrow Tobin Street leads to the Triskel Arts Centre, with exhibitions of contemporary arts and

crafts, as well as film and stage shows.
Follow Tobin St to Grand Parade.

6 Grand Parade

Spacious Grand Parade runs from crescent-shaped St Patrick's Street, Cork's main thoroughfare, to the south channel of the River Lee. About halfway along – close to where Tobin Street emerges – is the entrance to the English Market, a covered area of traditional stalls selling fresh grocery products and a pleasant café serving cakes upstairs.
Turn left into South Mall.

7 South Mall

The start of South Mall is marked by a memorial to Irish patriots. Across the road, the roof of the Allied Irish Bank is supported by six marble pillars from Old St Paul's, London.
Turn left into Princes St and right into St Patrick's St, completing the walk at St Patrick's Bridge.

Cork is a delightful waterside city connected by bridges crossing the River Lee

Flora and fauna

Ireland preserves natural habitats which have disappeared from the rest of Europe. Naturalists from all over the world visit unique locations like The Burren to see Arctic and Mediterranean plants growing side by side. They travel to rocky islands, rich wetlands and areas still farmed traditionally to observe huge concentrations of migratory birds and species that have become rare in other countries – like the corncrake and the chough.

You are never far from the countryside in Ireland. A well-marked 3km (2-mile) nature trail lies within 3km (2 miles) of Belfast city centre – at Lagan Meadows, starting at the Knightsbridge Park entrance. Here you can see kingfishers, snipe, woodcocks, reed buntings and herons.

The National Trust has built several bird hides at Strangford Lough. Migrant geese, ducks, shorebirds and seabirds gather

Hinds at Killarney National Park

Large tracts of relatively undisturbed natural landscape, such as The Burren, allow wildlife a sanctuary and visitors some rare sightings

here by the thousands at different seasons (*see p108*).

Rathlin Island, off the north coast, attracts serious ornithologists with its extensive sanctuary at Kebble. Huge numbers of birds – puffins, razorbills, fulmars and guillemots – sit wing to wing on cliff ledges and rock stacks, raucously shrieking (*see p124*). In Glenveagh National Park, golden eagles were recently reintroduced.

Otters thrive all over Ireland. Native red deer, pine martens, red squirrels, grey seals, dolphins, wild goats and hares are among mammals regularly seen.

Cape Clear, an island off Co Cork, has an observatory built by Bristol University from which rare songbird migrants are seen, as well as seabirds (*see p125*).

The nutrient-poor boglands sustain many small plants – deer sedge, bog cotton, bog rosemary, bog asphodel – and insects. Sundews, butterworts and bladderworts trap insects for sustenance.

The Burren, in Co Clare, is a vast, waterless plateau of limestone hills, drawing geologists and botanists, especially in May, when countless colourful flowers appear.

An unusual feature of Drombeg is its communal cooking pit in which some 340 litres (75 gallons) of water could be boiled by throwing in hot stones. A TV cook has successfully cooked a joint of meat there, using the Stone Age method.

On the R597, which loops back on to the N71 just before Leap, 3km (2 miles) west of Ross Carbery. Freely accessible.

Fota Wildlife Park

Giraffes, kangaroos, oryxes and monkeys wander freely among penguins, flamingos and peacocks, while an informal arboretum features exotic trees from all over the world. The 30-hectare (74-acre) park specialises in the breeding of certain endangered species.

Fota Island, Cork Harbour, on the N25, 13km (8 miles) east of Cork. Also reached by train from Cork. Tel: (021) 481 2678. www.fotawildlife.ie. Open: mid-Mar–mid-Nov Mon–Sat 10am–6pm, Sun 11am–6pm; mid-Nov–mid-Mar Mon–Sat 10am–4.30pm, Sun 11am–4.30pm. Admission charge.

Garinish Island

Rare subtropical plants jostle with rhododendrons, azaleas, climbing shrubs and herbaceous perennials on this colourful island in Bantry Bay, a favourite with George Bernard Shaw. The beautiful Italianate gardens, with colonnades, pools and terraces, as well as a wild garden, were laid out between 1810 and 1913.

Drombeg Stone Circle is one of the best-preserved monuments of its kind in Ireland

Reached in 10 mins by boat from Glengarriff. Tel: (027) 63040. Open: Apr Mon–Sat 10am–5.30pm, Sun 1–6pm; May & Sept Mon–Sat 10am–6pm, Sun noon–6pm; Jun Mon–Sat 10am–6pm, Sun 11am–6pm; Jul & Aug Mon–Sat 9.30am–6pm, Sun 11am–6pm; Oct Mon–Sat 10am–4pm, Sun 1–5pm. Admission charge. Last landing 1 hr before closing. Ferry charge. Harbour Queen Ferries tel: (027) 63116. www.harbourqueenferry.com. Blue Pool Ferry tel: (027) 63333. www.bluepoolferry.com

Lisselan Gardens

Interesting walks through 12 hectares (30 acres) of gardens and woodland. Lots of unusual plants to enjoy in this Robinsonian-style garden.

Lisselan, Clonakilty. Tel: (023) 883 3249. www.lisselan.com. Open: daily 8am–dusk. Admission charge.

FAMINE AND EMIGRATION

Cobh, formerly known as Queenstown, was the embarkation point for thousands of emigrants – many of them victims of the appalling famine years of 1845–8 when Ireland's potato crop repeatedly failed as a result of blight. Facing starvation, over a million people left the country for good, seeking a new life in Australia, Canada, New Zealand and the United States, setting up huge Irish communities overseas.

Old Midleton Distillery

The story of whiskey, the mystical spirit perfected by Irish monks in the 6th century, is told in the old stone buildings of a distillery, complete with the world's largest copper still, a cast-iron mill wheel, traditional craft displays – and a generous tot at the end of the tour.

Signposted from the N25 at Midleton, 19km (12 miles) east of Cork. Tel: (021) 461 3594. www.jameson whiskey.com. Open: Apr–Oct daily 10am–4.30pm; Nov–Mar daily

11.30am, 1pm, 2.30pm & 4pm. Tours only. Admission charge.

St Finnbarr's Cathedral

The 19th-century French Gothic cathedral, with its three spires, stands on the site of a 6th-century monastery founded by St Finbarr, who also founded Cork in the early part of the 7th century (*see p71*).

Bishop St, Cork. Tel: (021) 496 3387. Open: daily 9.30am–5.30pm. Donations welcome.

Shandon Steeple (St Anne's Church)

Dominating the skyline on the north side of the River Lee in Cork, the steeple of St Anne's Church invites those who climb the 37m (121ft) structure to choose a tune to be played on the carillon.

Church St, Shandon. Tel: (021) 450 5906. Open: Apr–Sept daily 10am–

Munster

Garinish's Italianate gardens: George Bernard Shaw wrote much of his play *St Joan* here

The greystone ruins of Timoleague Abbey, once Ireland's largest friary

5.30pm; Oct–Mar daily 10am–3.30pm. Admission charge.

Timoleague Abbey/ Castle Gardens

Timoleague Abbey was founded in 1240 and is one of Ireland's best-preserved early Franciscan friaries. Among the country's largest and most important religious houses, the monks here once traded as importers of Spanish wine.

Overlooking the abbey, palm trees and other exotic trees and shrubs flourish in beautiful walled gardens which embrace the scant ruins of 13th-century Timoleague Castle.

Signposted in the village of Timoleague. Abbey: freely accessible. Castle gardens: tel: (023) 46116. Open: Easter weekend & mid-May–mid-Sept daily noon–6pm. Admission charge.

CO KERRY

County Kerry has some of Ireland's most dramatic scenery, from the famous Ring of Kerry drive to the rugged mountains of Killarney National Park. Don't miss the Dingle Peninsula with its Iron Age fort and curious beehive huts.

The Blasket Centre

Provides an insight into Irish-language culture and life on Blasket Island. (*See p186 for ferries to the island.*) *Dunquin. Tel: (066) 915 6444. Open: Apr–Oct daily 10am–6pm. Admission charge.*

Derrynane House

The home of Daniel O'Connell, the 'Liberator', is now kept as a museum and memorial to the great 19th-century politician. The National Historic Park surrounding the house covers 120 hectares (297 acres) of subtropical plants, shrubs and coastal trees. There is also a nature trail, and visitors can bathe in the sea (*see Cahersiveen p81*). *Signposted off the N70, 1.5km (1 mile) north of Caherdaniel. Tel: (066) 947 5113. www.heritageireland.ie. Open: Apr–Sept daily 10.30am–6pm; Oct–late Nov Wed–Sun & public holidays 10.30am–5pm. Last admission 45 mins before closing. Admission charge to house; grounds freely accessible.*

Dunbeg Fort

Perched on a promontory above Dingle Bay, this Iron Age fort is protected on its landward side by trenches and a 7m (23ft)-thick wall. *On the R559 near Fahan, about 6km (4 miles) west of Ventry. Free admission.*

Gallarus Oratory

Amazingly pristine, the oratory is a perfect example of early Irish building, (8th or possibly 7th century). Completely unmortared, it has remained watertight for 1,200 years. *Off the R559, between Ballyferriter & Ballynana. Free admission.*

Kerry County Museum

This museum includes the Medieval Experience, which has a 'time car' trip back to medieval Tralee. *Ashe Memorial Hall, Denny St, Tralee. Tel: (066) 712 7777. www.kerry museum.ie. Open: Jan–May & Oct–Dec Tue–Sat 9.30am–5pm; Jun–Sept daily 9.30am–5.30pm. Admission charge.*

Kilmalkedar Church

This ruined 12th-century church is in the Romanesque style. The narrow east window is known locally as 'the eye of the needle', through which those seeking salvation must pass.

Muckross House

Off the R559, near the Gallarus Oratory. Free admission.

Muckross Abbey and House

Despite vandalism by Cromwell's troops in 1652, the 15th-century Franciscan abbey remains in a good state of preservation. Not far from the abbey is Muckross House, built in the 19th century in Elizabethan style. Its upper floors house a collection of documents, and there is a wildlife and bird exhibition. The house also incorporates the Kerry Folklife Centre, and nearby are the three working Muckross Traditional Farms. *On the N71 Kenmare road, 6km (4 miles) outside Killarney. Abbey open: daily during daylight hours. Free admission. House tel: (064) 667 0144. www.muckross-house.ie. Open: Jul & Aug daily 9am–7pm; Sept–Jun daily 9am–5.30pm. Admission charge. Shops open: daily 9am–5.30pm. Farms open: Mar, Apr & Oct Sat–Sun; May–Sept daily.*

Skellig Experience

This interpretive centre explores the history and archaeology of Skellig

Michael's early Christian monastery, its lighthouse service and local wildlife. *Boat from Valentia Island, which is accessed by road bridge from Portmagee. Tel: (066) 947 6306. www.skellig experience.com. Open: Mar, Apr & Oct daily 10am–5pm; May, Jun & Sept daily 10am–6pm; Jul & Aug daily 10am–7pm. Admission charge. Book ahead during peak season.*

CO LIMERICK

Ireland's longest river, the Shannon, marks the northern boundary of County Limerick, the nation's western gateway. Like County Clare on the opposite bank, it is dotted with medieval castles and striking scenery.

Foynes Flying Boat Museum

The focal point for aircraft crossing the north Atlantic in the 1930s and 1940s, the old terminus building, radio and weather rooms are on show, with original equipment. An audiovisual presentation is given in a 1940s-style cinema, and there is a tea room.
On the N69, Foynes, about 24km (15 miles) west of Limerick. Tel: (069) 65416. www.flyingboatmuseum.com. Open: end Mar–Oct daily 9am–5pm. Admission charge.

Limerick
The Hunt Museum

This museum houses one of Ireland's greatest private collections of art and antiquities. Wander round and find a

Picasso, a Renoir, a Da Vinci, a Sheela-na-gig, a bishop's crozier, an ancient pot and thousands of other pieces – all donated to the Irish people by John and Gertrude Hunt.
Custom House, Rutland St, Limerick. Tel: (061) 312833. www.huntmuseum. com. Open: Mon–Sat 10am–5pm, Sun 2–5pm. Admission charge.

King John's Castle

Imaginative models and displays interpret Limerick's 800-year history. Battlement walkways along the castle walls and towers provide wonderful views of the city, the River Shannon and surrounding countryside.
Nicholas St, Limerick. Tel: (061) 360788. www.shannonheritage.com. Open: daily 10am–5pm. Admission charge.

St Mary's Cathedral

Built as a palace in the 12th century, the cathedral (Protestant) still shows original architectural features. Misericords in the choir stalls, from the 15th century, bear grotesque carvings.
Bridge St, Limerick. Tel: (061) 310293. Free admission.

Lough Gur Heritage Centre

The area around Lough Gur is one of Ireland's most important archaeological sites, with numerous megalithic remains – stone circles, dolmens, wedge-shaped gallery graves and the sites of Neolithic dwellings. A wealth of artefacts has been discovered in

and around the lake. An audiovisual presentation of the Lough Gur story is given in the 'Neolithic-style' interpretative centre.
Off the R512 to Kilmallock, signposted 17km (10¹/₂ miles) south of Limerick. Tel: (061) 385186. www.loughgur.com. Open: Tue–Fri noon–5pm, Sat & Sun noon–7pm. Admission charge.

CO CLARE
Aillwee Cave
Hollows scraped out on the floor of the huge cave provide evidence of early occupation by the brown bear. The cave, one of the oldest in Ireland, estimated at 2 million years old, has a river, waterfall and well-lit passages.
3km (2 miles) south of Ballyvaughan. Tel: (065) 707 7036. www.aillweecave.ie. Open: daily 10am–6pm; late Nov–Dec by appointment. Admission charge.

Bunratty Castle and Folk Park
A restored Norman-Irish keep built in 1277, the castle houses a fine collection of furniture and furnishings from the 14th to the 17th centuries. Medieval banquets are a twice-nightly feature throughout the year. The Folk Park, in the castle grounds, is a reconstructed 19th-century street.
On the N18, 12km (7¹/₂ miles) northwest of Limerick. Tel: (061) 360788. www.shannonheritage.com. Open: Jun–Aug Mon–Fri 9am–5.30pm, Sat & Sun 9am–6pm; Sept–May daily 9am–5.30pm. Last admission to castle 4pm. Admission charge.

The Burren
A unique rocky landscape with rare botany. Visit the excellent **Burren Centre** before you set off to explore. Highlights include the Poulnabrone dolmen and Kilfenora Cathedral.
Kilfenora. Tel: (065) 708 8030. www.theburrencentre.ie. Open: mid-Mar–May & Sept–mid-Oct daily 10am–5pm; Jun–Aug daily 9.30am–5.30pm.

Cliffs of Moher
These sheer cliffs rising over 215m (700ft) from the ocean's edge and stretching for almost 8km (5 miles) along the coast are western Ireland's most dramatic beauty spot. There are spectacular views from O'Brien's Tower.
Off the R478, north of Liscannor. Tel: (065) 708 6141. www.cliffsofmoher.ie. Open: Mar & Oct 9am–6pm; Apr 9am–6.30pm; May & Sept 9am–7pm; Jun 9am–7.30pm; Jul & Aug 9am–9pm (from 15 Aug until 8pm); Nov–Feb 9.15am–5pm; see website for weekend & holiday hrs. Admission charge.

Craggaunowen, The Living Past
Many skills have been revived in this project in the grounds of a restored 16th-century castle. The most dramatic reconstruction is that of a crannog, a Bronze Age lake dwelling. A replica of St Brendan's 6th-century leather boat is also on show.
Off the R469, 10km (6 miles) south of Quin. Tel: (061) 360788. www.shannon heritage.com. Open: mid-Apr–Aug daily 10am–4.15pm. Admission charge.

Tour: The Ring of Kerry

Justifiably the most popular excursion in Ireland, the 170km (106-mile) Ring of Kerry is a dramatic experience: a mix of rugged moorland and mountains, lakes, rivers and streams, cliffs, beaches and weather-beaten islands.

Allow 1 day.

Begin at the town of Killarney.

1 Killarney

A comparatively modern town – it sprang into prominence in the 18th century – Killarney is a lively place where jaunting cars (horse-drawn carriages) and coaches compete.

Follow the N71 southwest for 18km (11 miles) to Ladies' View.

2 Ladies' View

The road soon weaves and climbs above the waters of Muckross Lake, and it is

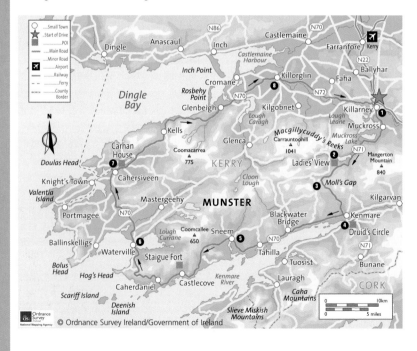

© Ordnance Survey Ireland/Government of Ireland

not difficult to understand the delight of Queen Victoria and her ladies-in-waiting, after whom the view is named. It is best seen from the second car park – a great panorama of the Killarney Valley.
Continue along the N71 for 5km (3 miles).

3 Moll's Gap

Another stunning viewpoint overlooks Macgillycuddy's Reeks and 1,041m (3,415ft)-high Carrauntoohill, Ireland's highest mountain. Moll's Gap has a restaurant and craft shop.
Continue south for 10km (6 miles).

4 Kenmare

The streets of Kenmare, reached after a drive across rugged mountain terrain, were laid out in an X-formation in 1775. The town has an ancient stone circle, known locally as the Druid's Circle, on the banks of the River Finnihy.
Take the N70 west for 27km (17 miles).

5 Sneem

The road follows the Kenmare River, and there are splendid views of the Caha and Slieve Miskish Mountains. Sneem, a pretty village with colourful painted houses surrounding a green, has good, safe beaches. Fishing for salmon and brown trout is popular.

Inland, 4km (2½ miles) from Castlecove on the N70, is the Staigue Fort, about 2,500 years old and one of Ireland's best-preserved ancient structures.
Continue on the N70 for 35km (22 miles) to Waterville.

6 Waterville

Waterville, best known today for its golf course and salmon fishing, is said to be the landing place of Noah's grandson Beith and granddaughter Cessair, who had failed to gain places on the Ark and had to build their own.
Drive north for 16km (10 miles).

7 Cahersiveen

Cahersiveen has strong associations with the patriot Daniel O'Connell. The Liberator's birthplace, Carhan House, is 1.5km (1 mile) north of the town. Cahersiveen is also the terminus for a ferry service to Valentia Island, which has 3,000km (1,864 miles) of ocean between it and Newfoundland.
Follow the N70 for 40km (25 miles).

8 Killorglin

The road skirts Dingle Bay, with views to the north of the Dingle Peninsula's peaks, and passes through the resort of Glenbeigh. Killorglin, a hillside town, is best known for its August Puck Fair, a festival based on a pagan custom.
Take the N72 southeast for 21km (13 miles) to complete the drive at Killarney.

Ladies' View

Connacht

Connacht, where Irish is a living language and University College Galway is a centre of Gaelic culture, has a range of beautiful scenery – from tranquil to wild and craggy. Its lakes and the shore of the River Shannon attract thousands of fishermen every year, and its extensive coastline caters for the sea angler, the yachtsman and the beach addict.

Co Galway

Lively Galway City combines a medieval atmosphere with a musical and cultural tradition which draws in young people from Europe and beyond each summer. Venture west into Connemara for stunning coastal scenery backed by wild mountains and expansive bogs inland.

Alcock and Brown Memorial

A cairn near the Marconi station ruins marks the place where intrepid aviators Alcock and Brown landed after the first non-stop transatlantic flight from St John's, Newfoundland, in 1919. On higher ground an aircraft monument marks the achievement.
Derrygimlagh Bog, 6km (4 miles) south of Clifden. Free admission.

Aran Islands

See p124.

Aughnanure Castle

Close to the shores of Lough Corrib, on rocky ground, this 16th-century Irish tower house, built by the O'Flahertys, stands six storeys high. The remains of a banqueting hall, a circular watchtower and a dry harbour can be seen. Many bats use the castle as a roost.
Oughterard. Tel: (091) 552214. www.heritageireland.ie. Open: end Apr–end Oct daily 9.30am–6pm. Admission charge.

Clonfert Cathedral

St Brendan founded a Benedictine monastery here in the 6th century. A superb Romanesque doorway is the highlight.
Clonfert. Free admission.

The Alcock and Brown Memorial

Connemara National Park

This 2,000-hectare (4,942-acre) area encompasses a range of habitats – heath, bogland, woodland and grassland – including four peaks of the Twelve Bens (Pins) mountain range. There are stunning views, and a well-established herd of Connemara ponies roams the park.

The visitor centre provides detailed information on walks and nature trails. *Letterfrack, Connemara. Visitor centre:* *tel: (095) 41054. Open: Mar–May, Sept & Oct daily 10am–5.30pm; Jun–Aug daily 9.30am–6.30pm. Free admission.*

Coole Nature Reserve

The grounds of Lady Augusta Gregory's former estate, Coole Park, have become a nature reserve. This unique matrix of habitats incorporates a nature trail, a forest and a lake, and is home to a herd of red deer and other animal and bird species. There is an

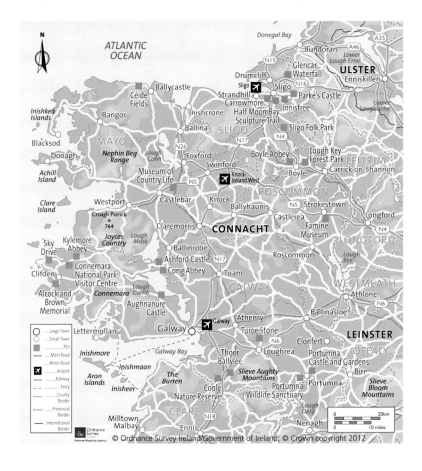

© Ordnance Survey Ireland/Government of Ireland; © Crown copyright 2012

interpretative centre which explains the role of the reserve, as well as picnic sites and tea rooms.

Gort. Tel: (091) 631804. www.coole park.ie. Open: mid-Apr–Jun & early–mid-Sept daily 10am–5pm; Jul & Aug daily 10am–6pm. Free admission.

Kylemore Abbey

This attractive lakeside abbey, originally built as a public residence, is now a convent for Benedictine nuns. Its Gothic chapel is a small-scale version of England's Norwich Cathedral. The 2.5-hectare (6-acre) Victorian walled garden, one of the most impressive in Ireland in its time, has been restored.

18km (11 miles) from Clifden. Tel: (095) 52000. www.kylemoreabbey.com. Open: Jan daily 11am–4pm; Feb daily 11am– 5pm; mid-Mar–Apr daily 9am–5.30pm; May–late Jun, Sept & Oct daily 9am– 6pm; late Jun–Aug daily 9am–7pm; Nov daily 10am–5pm; Dec daily 10am–4.30pm.

Portumna Castle and Gardens

A partially restored, 17th-century fortified house, the ground floor of the castle and the formal gardens are open to visitors. The walled kitchen garden has been completely restored. Beside the castle are the well-preserved ruins of Portumna Priory, built in 1254.

Portumna. Tel: (090) 974 1658. Open: end Apr–Sept daily 9.30am–6pm; Oct Sat & Sun 9.30am–5pm. Admission charge.

Kylemore Abbey

Portumna Wildlife Sanctuary

Portumna Forest Park, run by the Forest and Wildlife Service, has 400 hectares (988 acres) of walks in what was formerly the Harewood Estate. Bordered along its southern edges by Lough Derg, the sanctuary is home to a variety of animals, including red and fallow deer. A nature trail leaflet is available.

Near Portumna town, approaching from Woodford. Freely accessible.

Sky Drive

The Sky Drive, 14km (9 miles) of narrow road high over Clifden Bay, is one of the most scenic stretches of Co Galway, circling the peninsula west of the town and opening up vast seascapes. This road is very popular with landscape painters.

Thoor Ballylee

This former summer house of W B Yeats, where he wrote most of his works, has been restored to look as it did in his time. The 16th-century tower house contains a display of first editions of his work, and visitors can 'climb the narrow, winding stair'. There is an audiovisual presentation of the poet's life, as well as a bookshop, craft shop and tea room, gardens and picnic area. *Gort. Tel: (091) 631436. Open: Jun–Sept Mon–Sat 9.30am–5pm. Admission charge.*

Co Mayo

Vast stretches of lonely bogland, stark headlands and pristine coastline cover much of County Mayo. In contrast, it draws thousands of pilgrims to St Patrick's mountain and the holy shrine at Knock.

Achill Island

Reached by a short causeway, Achill Island is the largest of Ireland's islands. There are weird rock formations in the cliffs flanking the 3km (2-mile) beach at Keel, and the Atlantic Drive provides excellent views of the foothills and sandy beaches.

Boats can be hired at Keel Harbour for shark and other big-game fishing or to enjoy the dramatic cliff scenery. Stone circles and dolmens dot the island. *Reached from Mulrany on the mainland.*

Céide Fields

An environmental interpretive centre, with audiovisual presentations, at this extensive Stone Age settlement where tombs, 5,000-year-old dwellings, rare plants and rock formations can be seen. *8km (5 miles) west of Ballycastle. Tel: (096) 43325. Open: mid-Apr–May & Oct daily 10am–5pm; Jun–Sept daily 10am–6pm. Guided tours of site. Admission charge.*

Clare Island

See pp124–5.

Cong Abbey

Completed in 1128 for the Augustinians, Cong Abbey replaced a former church built during the 6th or 7th century and destroyed by Norsemen. It was founded by Turlough O'Connor, High King of Ireland, whose son, Roderick, the last High King, died in the abbey in 1198. The restored

The North Doorway, Cong Abbey

cloister and the monks' fishing house can still be seen. The village of Cong was the location for the 1952 John Wayne film *The Quiet Man*.
Cong, between Lough Mask & Lough Corrib. Free admission.

Croagh Patrick

Known locally as the *reekh*, this craggy mountain dominates the scenery around Westport. It is Ireland's holiest mountain as St Patrick fasted on the summit for 40 days. On the last Sunday in July over 20,000 pilgrims climb the mountain and Mass is celebrated on the hour. Some of the pilgrims climb barefoot. It is a tough climb, but the views on a clear day are spectacular.
On the R335 at Murrisk, 10km (6 miles) southwest of Westport. Tel: (098) 64114. Visitor centre open: Apr–Oct daily. Free admission.

Foxford Woollen Mills Visitor Centre

The story of this 19th-century working mill, from the famine years to the present day, is told through a captivating animated presentation.
Foxford. Tel: (094) 925 6104. www. foxfordwoollenmills.com. Open: Mon–Sat 10am–6pm, Sun noon–6pm. Tour every 20 mins. Free admission.

Inishkea Islands

These two low-lying, exposed islands form a sanctuary for up to 60 per cent of the Irish winter population of barnacle geese – some 2,900 birds.
4km (2½ miles) west of Belmullet Peninsula.

Knock Shrine

Pilgrims from around the world flock to Knock, where apparitions of the Virgin Mary were reported in 1879. Since then,

Croagh Patrick above pretty Westport town

it has been regarded as the Lourdes of Ireland. A 20,000-seat circular church was built at the site in 1976 to accommodate the huge pilgrimages.
On the N17, Knock, 15km (9¹/₂ miles) south of Ireland West Airport. Tel: (094) 938 8100. www.knock-shrine.ie. Free admission.

Museum of Country Life

Award-winning, purpose-built museum set in the parklands of Turlough Park. The museum concerns itself with the daily lives of ordinary people and its rooms are filled with furniture, agricultural implements, clothing, boats and simple country machinery such as looms and spinning wheels, horse-drawn mowing machines and butter churns. In addition, there is some original film footage of now-lost traditions and skills.
Turlough. Tel: (094) 903 1755. www.museum.ie. Open: Tue–Sat 10am–5pm, Sun 2–5pm. Free admission.

Westport House

One of the most stately homes of Ireland, this handsome Georgian mansion, begun in 1730, was completed in 1788 for the Marquess of Sligo on the site of an earlier castle whose dungeons still exist. The architect was Richard Castle, whose work was remodelled by James Wyatt. It is a place of contrasts – antique silver, Waterford glass, Georgian and Victorian furniture and family portraits by Reynolds are on display, while video games flash in the dungeons. Ireland's premier family leisure park is set up in the small lakeside grounds.
Near The Quay, Westport. Tel: (098) 27766. www.westporthouse.ie. Open: Apr–Jun & Sept daily 10am–4pm; Jul & Aug daily 10am–5.30pm; Oct–Dec some weekends. Admission charge.

Westport town

Westport was designed by the architect James Wyatt and built on land owned by the Marquess of Sligo. With an octagonal centre, lime trees either side of a canalised river, Clew Bay at its feet and a wealth of grand Georgian buildings, it attracts many visitors.

The Thursday-morning market at the Octagon brings the farmers into town.

Co Sligo

County Sligo is best known as Yeats Country, and its beautiful landscapes inspired one of Ireland's most famous poets. Its rolling hills and fields are also littered with thousands of prehistoric sites, while Sligo town is renowned for its traditional music.

Carrowmore

The largest cemetery of megalithic tombs in Ireland can be seen at the top of a mountain at Carrowmore. More than 60 tombs, a variety of dolmens, passage graves and stone circles extend over half a square kilometre. One of the tombs dates back more than 6,000 years, while the Bronze Age standing
(Cont. on p90)

Country life

Rural existence is still the way of life for a large proportion of Irish people. Apart from the conurbations with six-figure populations – Dublin, Cork, Limerick and Belfast – towns are small islands of activity in a brilliant green landscape, where agriculture makes a vital contribution to the economy.

Migration into the cities to find work has diminished some rural populations. In other cases urban sprawl has eroded the rural way of life.

Farming, forestry and fishing are important industries in Northern Ireland. So it is no surprise that such events as showjumping, horse racing, agricultural shows and ploughing matches attract huge numbers of spectators, or that hunting, shooting and fishing are pursuits enjoyed by many thousands.

Small fields enclosed by low stone walls give way to open, rich reddish-brown bogland, or tiny rural main-road villages. Barley, wheat, sugar beets and

Farmhouse at sunset, Co Antrim

Fishing in River Lackagh, Cresslough, Donegal

potatoes grow well in the rich, moist soil, but it is sheep and cattle rearing and dairy products that represent most of the agricultural output. Even on busy main roads motorists must be prepared to encounter a herd of cows or flock of sheep.

Living in isolated farms and cottages, the people are nevertheless gregarious, enjoying the social, sporting and cultural life to be found in bars and church halls, dance halls and playing fields.

On market days the country goes to town. Jam-packed at the bar after several hours of dealing, the farming fraternity, exuding a heady smell of damp tweed, presents a haze of flat caps, gleaming gaiters, gnarled, knowing faces and sage comments.

stones are thought to be from 1750 BC. A visitor centre contains an exhibition about Stone Age man and the excavations.

On the R292, 5km (3 miles) west of Sligo, east of Knocknarea Hill. Visitor centre: tel: (071) 916 1534. Open: Easter–mid-Oct daily 10am–6pm. Admission charge.

Drumcliff Monastic Site

Little is left of this 6th-century settlement except the stump of a round tower on one side of the N15 road and an elaborately carved 1,000-year-old high cross on the other (*see p96*). The carvings on the cross depict a selection of biblical scenes. (*See p91 for Yeats's grave.*)

7.5km (4¹/₂ miles) north of Sligo. Good visitor centre & café by the church. Freely accessible.

Half Moon Bay Sculpture Trail

A unique collection of wooden sculptures is scattered throughout Hazelwood Forest, on the northern shore of Lough Gill. The sculptures range from figures from Irish legend to Art Nouveau forms by Irish and foreign sculptors, and can be seen by following forest trails starting at the car park.

Off the Dromahair road, Hazelwood Forest, 3km (2 miles) from Sligo. Freely accessible.

Inishcrone (Enniscrone)

Seaweed found at this seaside resort, 53km (33 miles) west of Sligo, by

Yeats's grave at Drumcliff

Killala Bay, is renowned for its curative properties. People travel from far and wide to submerge themselves in the hot, seaweed-enriched salt water at the town's bathhouses. Just north of the town is the Valley of Diamonds – a shell collector's paradise.

Kilcullen's Seaweed Baths, Inishcrone. Tel: (096) 36238. Open: times vary. Admission charge.

Innisfree

There are daily boat trips from Sligo town and Parke's Castle (*see p93 & p97*) to this Lough Gill island, immortalised by the poet Yeats. But those content to look from a distance can see it from the shore.

Lough Gill, east of Sligo. Boat trips: Wild Rose Water Bus. Tel: (071) 916 4266 for schedule. Freely accessible.

CASTLEREA

Castlerea is Co Roscommon's third-largest town, and is known mainly as the birthplace, in 1815, of Sir William Wilde, the father of Oscar.

Sligo Folk Park

Life in 19th-century Ireland is re-created in a series of buildings: the old forge (still working), a rural cottage and farmyard, a bigger house, and the museum itself. It is a typical village street, complete with all the things that would have been on sale. There is also a schoolroom, and several workshops where furniture and artefacts are being restored.
Millview House, Riverstown. Tel: (071) 916 5001. www.sligofolkpark.com. Open: May–Sept Mon–Sat 10am–5pm, Sun 12.30–6pm; Oct–Apr Mon–Fri 10am–5pm. Admission charge.

Strandhill

Strandhill is a quiet seaside village with a good beach and excellent facilities for surfing, but swimming is not safe.

Dolly's Cottage, a small folk museum housed in a 19th-century dwelling, sells home-made produce and sometimes holds evening traditional music sessions.
Strandhill, near Sligo Airport. Dolly's Cottage open: summer afternoons. Free admission.

Yeats's grave

Although he died in Roquebrune, France, W B Yeats was eventually buried at Drumcliff. Tidily maintained, the plain grave of the poet lies within the shadow of the flat-topped Benbulben Mountain. The headstone bears an inscription from his final poem:

> *Cast a cold Eye*
> *On Life, on Death.*
> *Horseman, pass by!*

There is a visitor centre outlining the history of the church and Drumcliff, and also a little shop and café.
On the N15, Drumcliff, 7.5km (4½ miles) north of Sligo. Grave freely accessible. Visitor centre: tel: (071) 914 4956. Open: Mon–Sat 9am–6pm, Sun noon–6pm. Admission charge.

Co Roscommon
Boyle Abbey

The impressive ruins of this Cistercian abbey show traces of their original splendour. The nave, with both Romanesque and Gothic arches, and the choir and transepts of the 12th-century church are still in good condition.
Boyle. Tel: (071) 966 2604. www.heritage ireland.ie. Open: Easter–Sept daily 10am–6pm. Admission charge.

Clonalis House

Clonalis is the ancestral home of the clan O'Conor, who claim to be Europe's oldest family, tracing their ancestry to AD 75. The 19th-century mansion has items associated with the family, including the harp of Irish musician Turlough O'Carolan (1670–1738).
Castlerea. Tel: (094) 962 0014.

Connacht

Open: Jun–Aug Mon–Sat 11am–5pm. Admission charge.

Famine Museum

The greatest Irish tragedy is memorialised in this museum in the stables of Strokestown House. It doesn't paint a good picture of the Whig British government's laissez-faire attitude. Strokestown Park House is a Palladian mansion with magnificent pleasure gardens designed by Richard Castle. It provides a good insight into the lives of the 19th-century Anglo-Irish gentry.

Strokestown. Tel: (071) 963 3013. www.strokestownpark.ie. Open: mid-Mar–Oct daily 10am–5.30pm. Admission charge.

Roscommon

The county's economy is still based on sheep and cattle, and Roscommon has one of Ireland's best weekly livestock markets. More notoriously, all the public hangings in Co Roscommon took place at Roscommon Gaol. One of the inmates long ago, the notorious 'Lady Betty', was found guilty of the murder of her son, but had her death sentence commuted on condition that she carried out all further hangings without reward. She accepted the deal, which is commemorated with a plaque.

Roscommon's Norman castle was built, captured by the Irish who razed it to the ground, and rebuilt all in the space of 11 years, from 1269 to 1280. Massive and roofless, though otherwise reasonably well preserved, it stands majestic, north of the town.

Just outside the town, on the road to Boyle, is the impressive ruin of **Roscommon Abbey**. This Dominican priory was founded in 1253 and somehow survived the religious persecution that followed the Reformation. Eight sculpted figures can be seen at the base of the tomb of Felim O'Conor, King of Connacht, in the remains of a substantial church. These figures depict gallowglasses – medieval Irish professional soldiers.

Co Leitrim
Carrick-on-Shannon

Though a small town, Carrick is the capital of Leitrim and has a lovely position on the River Shannon. The Marina is a hub of activity in summer and a number of companies rent out cruisers.

Glencar Waterfall

From the N16 Manorhamilton to Sligo road you will see the 17m (56ft)-high waterfall tumbling in an unbroken leap into Glencar Lough long before the right turn that leads you to it. There are several waterfalls nearby, but this is the highest. It is this waterfall that Yeats immortalised in his poem *The Stolen Child*.

East of Drumcliff. Freely accessible.

Lough Key Forest Park

Close to the county capital, Carrick-on-Shannon, this forest park lies along the banks of Lough Key. It has nature trails, bog gardens, a canal walk, boating facilities and a restaurant. Climb to the high ground, known as Moylurg Tower, for views of the surrounding countryside and the islands dotted across the lake.

On the N4, east of Boyle. www. loughkey.ie. Freely accessible; charge for car park.

Parke's Castle

This strongly fortified 17th-century manor house was the home of an Englishman, Robert Parke, who undiplomatically dismantled a neighbouring castle to provide the material to build his own. The castle had been owned by the powerful

CO LEITRIM

Leitrim is Ireland's least-populated county. Its largest town, Carrick-on-Shannon, has a population of fewer than 2,000. Anglers appreciate its many lakes and rivers, including a large section of the Shannon.

O'Rourke clan, and as a result Parke's home needed to be impregnable as a defence against the outraged Irish. The last residing O'Rourke harboured a Spanish Armada officer and was executed for treason. A video presentation relates the story, and there is a guided tour (*see p97*).

North of Dromahair, on the north shore of Lough Gill. Tel: (071) 916 4149. Open: Apr–Sept daily 10am–6pm. Admission charge.

Lough Key is the star attraction in the picturesque forest park

Walk: Galway City

Prosperous, vibrant and compact, historic Galway is ideal for touring on foot.

Allow 1½ hours.

Begin on the southeast side of Eyre Square, in front of Hotel Meyrick, formerly the Galway Great Southern Hotel (the rail and bus stations are behind the hotel, on Station Rd).

1 Old medieval wall

Eyre Square is Galway's main gathering place. The wall can be seen on the south side, beside the Eyre Square shopping centre.

Pass through the shopping centre to William St and continue to Abbeygate St.

2 Lynch's Castle

The Allied Irish Bank on the corner of Shop Street and Abbeygate Street is

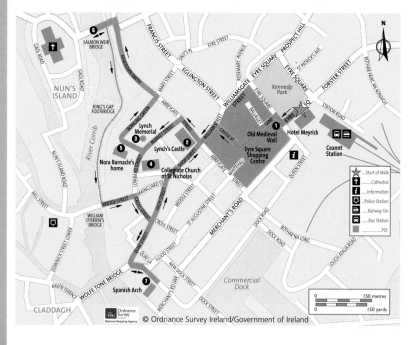

© Ordnance Survey Ireland/Government of Ireland

Looking north over Eyre Square

the best-preserved example of a
merchant's town castle.
*Turn right into Abbeygate St and left into
Market St.*

3 Lynch Memorial

An inscription on black marble set
above a Gothic doorway marks the
spot where, so local legend says, a 16th-
century mayor of Galway found his
own son guilty of murder, then hanged
the boy himself when the executioner
refused to carry out the sentence.
Continue to Lombard St.

4 Collegiate Church of
St Nicholas

Built by the Anglo-Normans in 1320
and enlarged in the 15th and 16th
centuries, the church has many fine
medieval carvings and relics.
Go back to Bowling Green and turn left.

5 Nora Barnacle's home

A memorial plaque marks the former
home of Nora Barnacle, James Joyce's
wife and inspiration for Molly Bloom in

Ulysses. The house is open to the public
in summer (*tel: (091) 564743; open: end
May–mid-Sept Tue–Sat 10am–1pm &
2–5pm; admission charge*).
*At the end of Bowling Green turn left
into Newtown Smith and continue to
where Salmon Weir Bridge crosses the
River Corrib.*

6 Salmon Weir Bridge

This bridge is the place from which
shoals of salmon can be seen as they
make their way upstream to spawn
from mid-April to early July.
*Follow the signed riverside walk to
William O'Brien's Bridge, bear left along
Bridge St, right into Cross St, and right
into Quay St to the Spanish Arch.*

7 Spanish Arch

Built in 1594, the arch once protected
the quays on which Spanish galleons
unloaded. Today, it adjoins the Galway
City Museum.
*Return along Quay St through the
shopping area of High St and Shop St to
complete the walk at Eyre Square.*

Tour: Yeats Country

W B Yeats was arguably Ireland's greatest poet. The distinctive profile of Benbulben broods over Sligo Bay and appears unexpectedly, ever changing in the area's capricious climate. The drive embraces some of the places where the poet found inspiration.

Allow 1 day.

Begin at Sligo town.

1 Sligo, Co Sligo

Sligo has a long and often violent history. In the 9th century it was attacked by the Vikings, followed by Irish and Anglo-Norman raiders. The only remains of its early days are the ruins of the 13th-century Dominican Abbey in Abbey Street. The Niland Collection in the Model Arts Centre on the Mall has many paintings by W B Yeats's father and brother. W B himself (1865–1939) is commemorated in the Sligo County Museum and the Yeats Memorial Building where the Yeats International Summer School is held every August. The Fiddler of Dooney competition, inspired by his poem, takes place at Sligo in July.
Take the N15 for 8km (5 miles).

2 Drumcliff, Co Sligo

The stump of a round tower and a 1,000-year-old high cross are all that remain of a monastery thought to have been founded by St Columba in the 6th century (*see p90*). Yeats's simple grave is to the left of the church entrance (*see p91*).
Continue on the N15 for 37km (23 miles) to Bundoran, then take the R280 for 5km (3 miles) to Kinlough.

3 Kinlough, Co Leitrim

An attractive village, Kinlough overlooks Lough Melvin and the ruins of Rossclogher Abbey.
Take the R281 along the south shore of Lough Melvin for 13km (8 miles). Turn right on to the R282 for 13km (8 miles) to Manorhamilton.

4 Manorhamilton, Co Leitrim

This workaday community was named after a 17th-century Scottish 'planter', Sir Frederick Hamilton, who built the now-ruined castle overlooking the town.
Follow the N16 west for about 13km (8 miles) to Glencar Lough.

5 Glencar, Co Leitrim

The N16 skirts the lake, presenting wonderful alpine views of the Glencar

Waterfall, immortalised in Yeats's poem *The Stolen Child* (*see p92*).
Continue along the N16 for about 16km (10 miles); turn left on the R286.

6 Parke's Castle, Co Leitrim

Parke's Castle (*see p93*) offers a superb view of Lough Gill. Yeats's Lake Isle of Innisfree (*see p90*) can be reached by boat.
Continue on the R286, then turn right on the R288 for Dromahair.

7 Dromahair, Co Leitrim

The village was laid out along the lines of a Somerset settlement by an English family, the Lane-Foxes.
Take the R287.

8 Dooney, Co Sligo

In Dooney Rock Forest Park, in a lovely corner of Lough Gill, you will find the 'twining branches' mentioned in Yeats's poem *The Fiddler of Dooney*.
From here take the N4 north to Sligo.

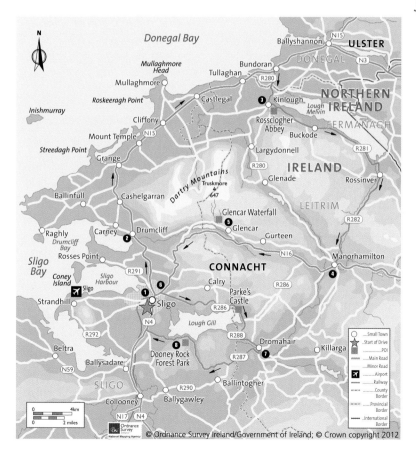

© Ordnance Survey Ireland/Government of Ireland; © Crown copyright 2012

Ulster

The ancient province of Ulster encompasses not only the six counties of Northern Ireland, but also Donegal, Cavan and Monaghan in the Republic. There is much to see here – the incredibly beautiful Sperrin Mountains, the Antrim Coast Road and the glorious lakeland of Fermanagh – or travel cross-country to Londonderry and Donegal where beauty is revealed round every corner.

Belfast

Belfast has so frequently been associated with the political troubles of Northern Ireland that it's often bypassed by visitors. In fact, it is a lively place with a handsome city centre, excellent restaurants and nightlife, an important arts festival and plenty of attractions from its historic opera house and Victorian saloon to its modern university and delightful botanic gardens.

Albert Memorial Clock Tower

Designed by W J Barre, this city icon is Belfast's leaning tower.
Queen's Square.

Belfast Zoo

On the lower slopes of Cave Hill, overlooking the city, the zoo has a lake with flamingos and a crannog, or fortified lake dwelling. There are red pandas, spectacled bears, rare tamarins and marmosets, sea lions and penguins.
Antrim Rd, 6.5km (4 miles) north of Belfast. Tel: (028) 9077 6277. www.belfast zoo.co.uk. Open: Apr–Sept daily 10am–7pm (last admission 5pm); Oct–Mar daily 10am–4pm (last admission 2.30pm). Admission charge.

Botanic Gardens

Dominated by the elegant covered-glass and cast-iron 1839 Palm House, these gardens include a Tropical Ravine.
Stranmillis Rd, Belfast 7. Tel: (028) 9032 4902. Open: daily dawn–dusk. Palm House & Tropical Ravine open: Apr–Sept daily 10am–noon & 1–5pm; Oct–Mar daily 10am–noon & 1–4pm. Last admission 15 mins before closing. Free admission.

Cave Hill Country Park

At the top of Cave Hill is MacArt's Fort, which includes a heritage centre. Rich in wild birds and plants, the hilltop also boasts great city views.
6.5km (4 miles) north of Belfast. Tel: (028) 9077 6925. Heritage centre open: Mon–Sat 9am–10pm, Sun 9am–5.30pm. Free admission.

City Hall

The City Hall (*see p102*) has a high dome based on St Paul's Cathedral in London. It cost less than £500,000 to build, and took eight years to construct, opening its doors on 1 August 1906. There are guided tours of the interior every day, including the Grand Staircase and the Great Hall, while outside the gardens with their statues are a popular spot for city workers and shoppers to take a break.

Donegall Square, Belfast 1. Tel: (028) 9027 0465. Open: Mon–Thur 8.30am–5pm, Fri 8.30am–4.30pm. Tours (advance bookings only): Mon–Fri 11am, 2pm & 3pm, Sat & Sun 2pm & 3pm. Free admission.

Crown Liquor Saloon

This ornate former railway hotel is one of Belfast's finest buildings (*see p103*). *46 Great Victoria St, Belfast 2. Tel: (028) 9027 9901. www.crownbar.com. Open: licensing hours.*

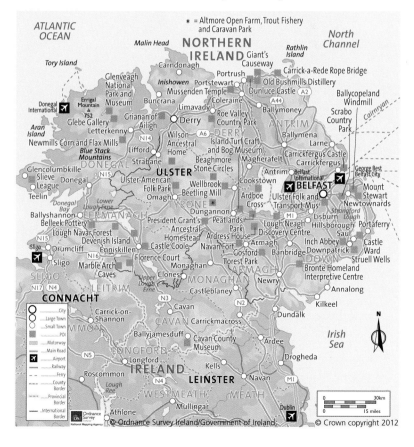

© Ordnance Survey Ireland/Government of Ireland. © Crown copyright 2012

Cultúrlann McAdam Ó Fiaich

A tourist information point for the Falls Road area of Belfast and a cultural centre with a programme of events.
216 Falls Rd. Tel: (028) 9096 4180. www.culturlann.ie. Open: daily 9am–10pm. Free admission.

Giant's Ring

An intriguing megalithic enclosure, the ring has a central dolmen encircled by a high, thick bank of earth. The site, thought to be 4,000 years old, was used for horse racing in the 18th century.
Off the B23, near Edenderry, south Belfast, via Ballynahatty Rd. Freely accessible.

Grand Opera House

Theatre, comedy, musicals and touring shows (*see p103*).
Great Victoria St, Belfast 1.

Belfast

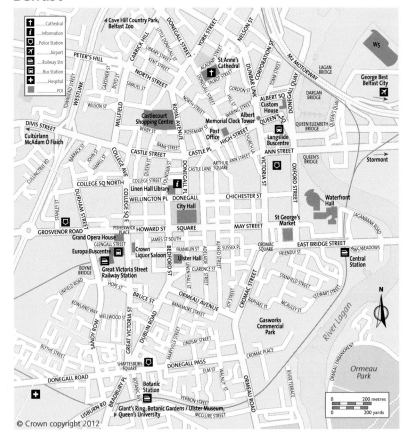

© Crown copyright 2012

Tel: (028) 9024 1919. www.goh.co.uk. Open: for performances.

Linen Hall Library
Thousands of old books stacked on shelves. A historical treasure trove.
17 Donegall Square North. Tel: (028) 9032 1707. www.linenhall.com. Open: Mon–Fri 9.30am–5.30pm, Sat 9.30am–4pm.

Queen's University
The architectural style of the main building, designed by Sir Charles Lanyon, with paved cloisters and a tower entrance, has echoes of Oxford's Magdalen College. The Queen's Visitor Centre contains memorabilia.
University Rd, Belfast 7. Welcome Centre: tel: (028) 9097 5252. Open: Mon–Fri 9.30am–4.30pm. Free admission.

St Anne's Cathedral
Building of this Anglican basilica in neo-Romanesque style began in 1899 and was completed 80 years later. Under the high nave lies Lord Edward Carson, opposer of Home Rule.
Donegall St, Belfast 1. Tel: (028) 9032 8332. www.belfastcathedral.org. Open: Sun–Fri 8am–4pm. Donations welcome.

St George's Market
A restored Victorian building, best visited on Friday or Saturday (market days) but often the venue for various events; good restaurant upstairs.
May St & Oxford St. Tel: (028) 9043 5704. www.stgeorgesmarket.com. Open:

Fri 6am–2pm, Sat 9am–3pm, Sun 10am–4pm. Free admission.

Stormont
Home to the Northern Ireland Assembly, this building is not open to the public, but people can wander in the parklands which line the 1.5km (1-mile) drive.
Off Newtownards Rd, Belfast 9, 10km (6 miles) east of the city. Grounds are open during daylight hours. Free admission.

Ulster Museum
This large collection covers art, archaeology and natural history, with displays ranging from dinosaurs and Egyptian mummies to works by Walter Sickert, Francis Bacon, Stanley Spencer, Bridget Riley and many more.
Botanic Gardens, Belfast 9. Tel: (028) 9044 0000. www.nmni.com/um. Open: Tue–Sun 10am–5pm. Free admission.

Waterfront Hall
This huge 2,000-seater concert hall offers fine views of the city from the glass-fronted galleries.
2 Lanyon Place. Tel: (028) 9033 4400. www.waterfront.co.uk. Open: Mon–Sat 10am–5pm.

W5
For children everywhere (and anyone who enjoys poking things to see what they can do), W5 is an interactive, science-nerd kind of place, with

(*Cont. on p106*)

Walk: Belfast's Golden Mile

This lively part of the city covers the area between Donegall Square and Shaftesbury Square. Though known as the Golden Mile, it covers less than 1km (²/₃ mile).

Allow 1¹/₂ hours.

Begin at Donegall Square.

1 Donegall Square

The eastern and western sides of the square form the terminus for city buses. The square itself is dominated by the

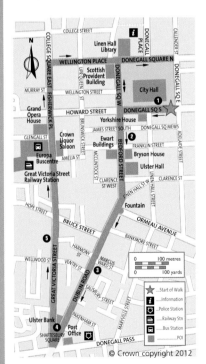

massive **City Hall** (*see p99*) and surrounded by the statues of civic worthies, including Sir Edward Harland, founder of the shipyard Harland and Wolff.

Queen Victoria gazes haughtily towards Donegall Place. Number 17 Donegall Square North is the Linen Hall Library, formerly a linen warehouse.

The Scottish Provident Building in Donegall Square West, another huge edifice, is decorated with looms, ships, spinning wheels and ropes, symbols of Belfast's traditional industries. Yorkshire House, at No 10 Donegall Square South, features the carved heads of notables such as Homer, Shakespeare and Michelangelo.

At the square's southwest corner follow Bedford St.

2 Bedford Street

In the 19th century this was the centre of the city's linen industry and the street was dominated by warehouses.

Among the survivors are the palatial Ewart Buildings (Nos 7–17) and the Venetian-style Bryson House at No 28. Ulster Hall, opened in 1861, was intended for grand social occasions but became a focal point for political rallies addressed by the likes of Parnell and Lloyd George.

Further on is a fountain erected as a memorial to a 19th-century physician who died after tireless service at the Home for Incurables.
Bear right into Dublin Rd.

3 Dublin Road

Dublin Road begins with an abundance of furniture shops and furnishing companies and ends with shops selling second-hand books, stamps and prints.
Continue into Shaftesbury Square.

4 Shaftesbury Square

Shaftesbury Square marks the beginning of Belfast's student quarter – Queen's University (*see p101*) is nearby – with lots of shops and good eating places. Formed by the conjunction of six major thoroughfares, it is Belfast's equivalent of Piccadilly Circus or Times Square. The two supine figures decorating the façade of the Ulster Bank are known locally as 'Draft' and 'Overdraft'. Next to the post office, on the east side, is Donegall Pass, one of six wide avenues laid across the 17th-century estate of the 3rd Earl of Donegall.
From the west side of Shaftesbury Square walk north along Great Victoria St.

5 Great Victoria Street

Once fashionably residential, this recently redeveloped commercial thoroughfare consists mainly of record shops, charity shops and restaurants.

Its stars, however, are the **Crown Liquor Saloon** and the **Grand Opera House**, the first opposite and the second alongside the Europa Hotel. Built around 1885, the Crown (*see p99*) is a wild extravagance of brilliant tiles, stained glass and panelled snugs – all intimately lit by gas lamps and restored by the National Trust. The Grand Opera House, another recent restoration, was opened in 1895 and now presents a wide-ranging programme (*see pp100–101*).
Continue into Fisherwick Place, then College Square East, turning right into Wellington Place to complete the walk back at Donegall Square North.

The imposing Belfast City Hall in Donegall Square

Walk: Belfast's shopping area

The city centre north of Donegall Square is Belfast's major shopping precinct, with many large stores and shopping malls. Largely pedestrianised, it has some intriguing side streets and alleys.

Allow 1½ hours.

Begin at Donegall Square North and proceed northwards along Donegall Place.

1 Donegall Place

Belfast's Victorian prosperity is reflected in the solid, ornate architecture of the buildings in Donegall Place. Notable examples are the pink-sandstone Marks & Spencer building, a linen warehouse when it was erected in 1869, and the copper domes of the former Robinson and Cleaver store.
Turn right into Castle Lane.

2 Castle Lane

Halfway along this pedestrianised lane, on the right, is Callender Street, the main depot for pressing, weighing and packing linen in the late 18th century. Calendering is the smoothing process that gives bleached linen its final sheen.
Continue to Arthur Square.

3 Arthur Square

The city's oldest square is named after Sir Arthur Chichester, the Elizabethan adventurer who received Belfast as a reward in 1603 for defeating the great Hugh O'Neill. With its bandstand, clock and buskers, the square today is a relaxing spot for shoppers.
Cross Corn Market and enter Ann St.

4 Ann Street

Ann Street allows a glimpse of 19th-century Belfast, when half the city's streets were small courts and 'entries' – narrow alleyways. Half a dozen of these can be seen on the left. Joy's Entry carries the name of the family that published Britain's first daily newspaper, the *Belfast News Letter*, in 1737.
Turn left into Pottinger's Entry.

5 Pottinger's Entry

This was a fashionable address in the 1820s when the entry had 34 houses. Today, it contains one of Belfast's classical saloon bars, the Morning Star, with its frosted-glass windows.
Turn right into High St.

6 High Street

On the corner of High Street and Victoria Street is the imposing Protestant Church of St George, completed in 1816. Its portico came from a palatial house that was intended as a home for Frederick Hervey, Earl Bishop of Derry, but, when he died, the house was dismantled and the portico moved to St George's. The nearby Albert Memorial Clock Tower tilts some 1.3m (4ft) from the vertical as a result of poor foundations.

Cross Victoria St to Queen's Square and on to Donegall Quay.

7 Donegall Quay

The large yellow Italianate building overlooking the River Lagan is Custom House, built between 1854 and 1857 by Sir Charles Lanyon, and easily the finest neoclassical building in Belfast.

From Donegall Quay turn left into Albert Square and continue into Waring St. Cross Bridge St to Rosemary St and turn left into Wine Cellar Entry.

8 Wine Cellar Entry

One of the city's oldest pubs, White's Tavern was opened in 1630 and rebuilt in 1790. An open fire and plush seating contribute to a welcoming atmosphere.

Continue to High St, turning right into Castle Place. At Donegall Place, turn left to return to the starting point of the walk.

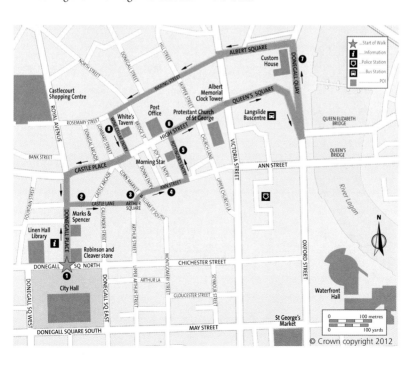

displays about gravity, electricity and how things work. Not just for children, this place can keep you busy for hours.
2 Queen's Quay. Tel: (028) 9046 7700. www.w5online.co.uk. Open: Mon–Fri 10am–5pm, Sat 10am–6pm, Sun noon–6pm. Last admission 1 hr before closing. Admission charge.

Co Down

To the south of Belfast, County Down borders Strangford Lough, home to grey seals and a variety of wildfowl. The southern part of the county is famous for the lovely Morne Mountains, and the sandy beaches at Newcastle.

Annalong Corn Mill

This early 19th-century water-powered mill, restored to working order, has an exhibition explaining the history of flour milling. There is also a herb garden, visitor centre, café and antiques shop.
Marine Park, Annalong. Tel: (028) 4376 8736. Visit by appointment. Admission charge.

Ark Open Farm

Nigerian pygmy goats, miniature horses, Jacob's sheep, rare breeds of pig and other creatures are featured at this small farm, along with a pets' corner and pony rides.
296 Bangor Rd, Newtownards. Tel: (028) 9182 0445. www.thearkopen farm.co.uk. Open: Apr–Oct Mon–Sat 10am–6pm, Sun 2–5pm; Nov–Mar Mon–Sat 10am–5pm, Sun 2–5pm. Admission charge.

Ballycopeland Windmill

This late 18th-century tower mill, which operated until 1915, is once again working. There is an electrically run model and a visitor centre.
On the B172, 1.5km (1 mile) west of Millisle. Tel: (028) 9186 1413. Open: Jul & Aug daily 10am–5pm. Free admission.

Brontë Homeland Interpretive Centre

Drumballyroney school and church is where Patrick Brontë, father of the three literary sisters, taught and preached before moving to Yorkshire. Now preserved, the centre marks the start of a 13km (8-mile) scenic drive, including Patrick's birthplace at Emdale.
Off the B10, 14km (9 miles) southeast of Banbridge. Tel: (028) 4063 1152. Open: Easter–Aug Fri–Sun noon–4.30pm; other times by prior arrangement. Admission charge.

Castle Ward

Very much a His and Hers house. He (Lord Bangor) wanted a classical Palladian home. She (his wife, Anne) wanted Strawberry Hill Gothic, which was all the rage in the 1760s. As a result, the front is classic, the back anything but. The marriage did not last, but the house, now a National Trust property, survives. Buildings include a corn mill, a sawmill, a dairy and a Victorian laundry. There is also a Victorian Pastimes Centre.
2.5km (1½ miles) west of Strangford. Tel: (028) 4488 1204. House open: mid-

Mar–Oct daily 11am–5pm. Estate open: daily 10am–dusk. Admission charge.

Down County Museum

Housed in a former gaol built in the late 18th century, this museum includes the St Patrick Heritage Centre, telling the story of the saint, plus local Stone Age artefacts and Bronze Age gold pieces.

The Mall, English St, Downpatrick. Tel: (028) 4461 5218. www.downcounty museum.com. Open: Mon–Fri 10am–5pm, Sat & Sun 1–5pm. Free admission.

Exploris

Many of the creatures that thrive in the waters of Strangford Lough (*see p108*) can be viewed – and some touched – in this sea aquarium.

The Rope Walk, Castle St, Portaferry. Tel: (028) 4272 8062. www.exploris. org.uk. Open: Apr–Aug Mon–Fri 10am–6pm, Sat 11am–6pm, Sun noon–6pm; Sept–Mar Mon–Fri 10am–5pm, Sat 11am–5pm, Sun 1–5pm. Admission charge.

Hillsborough Fort

Built in 1650, Hillsborough Fort was remodelled in the 18th century. Across the road is Hillsborough Castle, which was the scene of the signing of the Anglo-Irish agreement in 1985, and is the former residence of the Governor of Northern Ireland.

Hillsborough. Tel: (028) 9268 3285. Fort open: Apr–Sept Tue–Sat 10am–6pm, Sun 2–6pm. Grounds open: until dusk. Free admission.

River Quoile near Downpatrick

Inch Abbey

This ruined 12th-century Cistercian abbey, in a lovely woodland setting in the Quoile marshes, is approached by a causeway. The monks at Inch were English, having come from Furness Abbey, Lancashire. The triple east window still stands.

Off the A7, 6km (4 miles) north of Downpatrick. Tel: (028) 9023 5000 (Historic Monuments). Free admission.

Mount Stewart

These magnificent gardens, created by Lady Londonderry in the 1920s, support an enormous plant collection which enjoys the mild climate. Each garden has a theme – the Italian garden, the Spanish garden, the Shamrock garden, the Peace garden. The house (a National Trust property) contains antique furniture from Europe, collections of porcelain and important paintings. The **Temple of the Winds**, where many locals take their wedding vows, is an 18th-century folly with views over Strangford Lough.

A20, 8km (5 miles) southeast of Newtownards on Portaferry Rd. Tel: (028) 4278 8387. House open: mid-Mar–Oct daily noon–6pm. Garden open: mid-Mar–Oct daily 10am–6pm. Temple of the Winds open: times vary. Admission charge.

St Patrick's grave

St Patrick is reputed to be buried near the site of an old round tower in the churchyard at Down Cathedral, along with the bones of St Brigid and St Columba. A granite slab covers the hole made by pilgrims' feet.

Downpatrick. Freely accessible.

Saul

St Patrick is thought to have landed near Saul when he arrived in Ireland in 432. From here he travelled the country, converting the Irish. The 1932 St Patrick's Memorial Church was built where there was reputedly once a barn in which the saint held services.

3km (2 miles) northeast of Downpatrick. Tel: (028) 4461 4922. Open: daily.

Scrabo Country Park

Built in 1857 as a memorial to the 3rd Marquis of Londonderry, Scrabo Tower now serves as a countryside centre with woodland walks, quarries and interesting wildlife. Visitors can climb the 122 steps to the top of the 41m (135ft)-high tower for outstanding views over Strangford.

Scrabo Rd, Newtownards. Tel: (028) 9181 1491. Tower open: Easter, summer & public holidays, call for opening times. Free admission to park & tower.

Strangford Lough

One of Europe's richest places for marine wildlife, this large sea inlet, studded with 120 islands, is home to hundreds of marine animal species – from molluscs and sponges to birds and large colonies of seals.

On the A20, south of Newtownards.

Mount Stewart's Italianate garden is one of the most outstanding in Ireland

Struell Wells

Four pagan wells, reputed to have healing powers, and first recorded in 1306, are fed by an underground stream. There are men's and women's bathhouses and a drinking well built around 1600. Mass is celebrated at the site at midsummer.

Off the B1, 2.5km (1½ miles) east of Downpatrick. Tel: (028) 9023 5000 (Historic Monuments). Free admission.

Ulster Folk and Transport Museum

Original farmhouses, cottages, watermills, a church, a school and village buildings were moved stone by stone and re-erected to form this highly acclaimed outdoor museum. Inside, the transport section ranges from donkey creels (burden baskets) to aircraft.

Cultra, Holywood, 11km (7 miles) east of Belfast. Tel: (028) 9042 8428.

www.uftm.org.uk. Open: Mar–Sept Tue–Sun 10am–5pm; Oct–Feb Tue–Fri 10am–4pm, Sat & Sun 11am–4pm. Admission charge.

Co Armagh

County Armagh lies to the south of Lough Neagh, which is the largest lake in the British Isles. It is thought that St Patrick founded his first church here, on the site of Armagh Cathedral, and it continues to be the seat of the Roman Catholic Church in Ireland today.

Ardress House

This 17th-century farmhouse has a fine 18th-century front and an elegant drawing room with superb neoclassical plasterwork. The grounds contain a cobbled farmyard with livestock, and a woodland walk – the Ladies' Mile – surrounds the estate.

On the B28 (Ardress Rd) at

Journey to the stars at the Armagh Planetarium

Annaghmore, 11km (7 miles) west of Portadown. Tel: (028) 8778 4753. Open: Mar–Jun & Sept Sat & Sun 1–6pm; Easter week daily 1–6pm; Jul & Aug Thur–Sun 1–6pm. Admission charge.

Armagh County Museum

City-centre museum with a miscellany of artefacts and changing exhibitions throughout the year.
The Mall East, Armagh. Tel: (028) 3752 3070. www.nmni.com. Open: Mon–Fri 10am–5pm, Sat 10am–1pm & 2–5pm. Free admission.

Armagh Friary

Set in the grounds of the Archbishop's Palace, this friary is the only evidence of medieval settlement in Armagh. It was founded for the Franciscans in 1263 by Archbishop Patrick O'Scanail.
Friary Rd, Armagh. Tel: (028) 3752 9629. Free admission.

Armagh Planetarium

Visitors can experience space travel through the latest hands-on computer exhibits in the planetarium's Hall of Astronomy. The planetarium theatre has a worldwide reputation for its innovative 'star shows' (booking advised). On display are astronomical instruments.
College Hill, Armagh. Tel: (028) 3752 3689. www.armaghplanet.com.
Open: Mon–Sat 10am–5pm. Shows every afternoon, see website for show times. Admission charge.

Gosford Forest Park

Several of the walks through the former demesne of Gosford Castle, in early 19th-century mock-Norman style, were devised by Jonathan Swift, author of *Gulliver's Travels*. Traditional breeds of poultry strut in open paddocks and ornamental pigeons coo in a dovecote. The estate also includes a deer park, walled garden and nature trail.
Gosford Rd, Markethill. Tel: (028) 3755 1277. www.gosford.co.uk. Castle closed to the public. Park open: daily 10am–dusk. Admission charge.

Lough Neagh Discovery Centre

This centre on Oxford Island has a wildlife exhibition and there are boat trips and talks on the flora and fauna of the Lough Neagh basin. Oxford Island is a birdwatcher's paradise with viewing hides and more than 8km (5 miles) of walks.
Exit 10 from the M1, Oxford Island. Tel: (028) 3832 2205. www.oxfordisland. com. Open: Mon–Fri 9am–5pm, Sat & Sun 10am–5pm. Free admission.

Navan Fort

The history and legends of the great Iron Age hill fort, which was once the ancient capital of the Kings of Ulster, are told here with the aid of computer technology in the visitor centre.
On the A28, 1.5km (1 mile) west of Armagh. Tel: (028) 3752 9644. Fort freely accessible. Visitor centre open: Apr–Sept daily 10am–7pm; Oct–Mar daily 10am–4pm. Admission charge.

Royal Irish Fusiliers Museum

This museum relates the regiment's history from 1793 to 1968. Exhibits include a soldier's uniform from the Peninsular War and a 1943 Christmas card from Adolf Hitler.
Sovereigns House, Mall East, Armagh. Tel: (028) 3752 2911. Open: Mon–Fri (including public holidays) 10am– 12.30pm & 1.30–4pm. Free admission.

St Patrick's Church of Ireland Cathedral

Believed by some to be the spot where St Patrick founded his first church, it has certainly been around since the 5th century. It is an entertaining little church, even if you're not a believer. Every old bit of stonework discovered over the last few centuries has been brought here and is leaning against the walls around the sides. Here is the Tandragee Man and a Sheela-na-gig,

St Patrick's Church of Ireland Cathedral

and the remains of an 11th-century high cross. The interior is filled with medieval carvings. Brian Ború is thought to be buried in the cathedral grounds.

Cathedral Close, Armagh. Tel: (028) 3752 3142. www.stpatricks-cathedral.org. Open: Apr–Oct daily 9am–5pm; Nov–Mar daily 9am–4pm. Donations accepted.

St Patrick's Trian

Three attractions in one are presented at this interpretive centre. The 'Armagh Story' traces developments from prehistoric times to the present day. 'The Least of All The Faithful' features St Patrick, who allegedly built a church here in the 5th century. The other attraction, of particular interest to children, celebrates 'The Land of Lilliput', based on Jonathan Swift's *Gulliver's Travels*. There is also a restaurant.

40 Upper English St, Armagh. Tel: (028) 3752 1801. Open: Mon–Sat 10am–5pm, Sun 2–5pm. Admission charge.

Co Monaghan
County Museum

Monaghan's county museum, housed in an 18th-century market house in the county town, is an award-winning museum with exhibits representing 200 years of local history, while pride of place goes to the 600-year-old bronze processional Cross of Clogher.

1–2 Hill St, Monaghan. Tel: (047) 82928. Open: Mon–Fri 11am–5pm, Sat noon–5pm. Free admission.

Co Cavan
Cavan County Museum

The former convent of the Sisters of Poor Clare, this interesting museum traces the history of the county from pre-Christian times to the present day.

Virginia Rd, Ballyjamesduff. Tel: (049) 854 4070. Open: Jul–Sept Tue–Sat 10am–5pm, Sun 2–6pm; Oct–Jun Tue–Sat 10am–5pm. Free admission.

Co Fermanagh

County Fermanagh is known as Ireland's lakeland. Fishing, boating and woodland walks are on offer, as well as a cave system and stately homes.

Belleek Pottery

Ireland's oldest pottery reveals the skills that produce its fine china and distinctive basketware. There are factory tours and visitors can take their time browsing in the museum, visitor centre and shop. The restaurant serves refreshments on fine Belleek tableware.

Belleek. Tel: (028) 6865 8501. www.belleek.ie. Visitor centre open: Jan & Feb Mon–Fri 9am–5.30pm; Mar–Jun Mon–Fri 9am–5.30pm, Sat 10am–5.30pm, Sun 2–5.30pm; Jul–Sept Mon–Fri 9am–6pm, Sat 10am–6pm, Sun noon–5.30pm; Oct–Dec Mon–Fri 9am–5.30pm, Sat 10am–5.30pm. Sun noon–5.30pm (Oct). Charge for tour.

Castle Coole

The stateliest of the National Trust's stately homes in Northern Ireland, Castle Coole was completed in 1798. It was designed by James Wyatt and built for the Earls of Belmore. The house has an imposing Palladian front and there are fine furnishings and plasterwork within. *On the A4, 2.5km (1½ miles) southeast of Enniskillen. Tel: (028) 6632 2690. www.nationaltrust.org.uk. House open: mid-Mar–late May & Sept Sat & Sun 11am–5pm; mid-Apr & Jun–Aug daily 11am–5pm. Grounds open: daily 10am–dusk. Admission charge.*

Devenish Island

This island has extensive monastic ruins and probably Ireland's most perfect round tower. The earliest ruins and the tower are 12th century, but the monastery was founded by St Molaise (d.563) and remained an important religious centre until the 17th century.

The Devenish ferry service was suspended in 2011 due to budget cutbacks. Contact Castle Archdale Country Park (*tel: (028) 6862 1588*) for further information and details of commercial boat tours.

Enniskillen Castle Museum

An impressive 15th-century castle overlooking Lough Erne. Great displays on Fermanagh history, wildlife and landscapes.
Castle Barracks, Enniskillen. Tel: (028) 6632 5000. www.enniskillencastle.co.uk. Open: Apr–Jun, Sept & Oct Mon & Sat 2–5pm, Tue–Fri 10am–5pm; Jul & Aug Tue–Fri 10am–5pm, Sat–Mon 2–5pm; Nov–Mar Mon 2–5pm, Tue–Fri 10am–5pm. Admission charge.

Florence Court

One of Ulster's most important 18th-century houses, Florence Court (*see p121*) was built by the Earls of Enniskillen. The house is noted for its extravagant rococo plasterwork and fine furniture. The surrounding forest park contains an ancient Irish yew tree, said to be the mother of all Irish yews.
Off the A4 & A32, 12km (7½ miles) southwest of Enniskillen. Tel: (028) 6634 8249. House open: mid-Mar– mid-Apr & Oct Sat & Sun 11am– 5pm; mid-end Apr, Jul & Aug daily 11am–5pm; May & Jun Wed–Mon 11am–5pm; Sept Sat–Thur 11am– 5pm. Grounds open: Mar–Oct daily 10am–7pm; Nov–Feb daily 10am–4pm. Admission charge.

Lough Navar Forest

Red deer and wild goats roam the forest, and a steep zigzag path, part of the Ulster Way, leads to views of Lough Erne, Co Donegal and Co Sligo.
Signposted off the A46, 8km (5 miles) northwest of Derrygonnelly. Tel: (028) 6634 3040. Open: daily 10am–dusk. Admission charge.

Enniskillen Castle

Marble Arch Caves

One of Europe's finest cave systems can be toured by electric boat and on foot in a 75-minute guided exploration of underground rivers, waterfalls, winding passages and huge chambers with impressive stalagmite and stalactite formations. Over 300 million years of history lie within a strange landscape of chasms and valleys. Take comfortable shoes and a sweater as it can get quite chilly. The visitor centre has an exhibition area, an audiovisual theatre and restaurant (*see p121*).

Following the A4 (Sligo road) and the A32, near Florence Court, 19km (12 miles) southwest of Enniskillen. Tel: (028) 6634 8855. www.marblearch caves.net. Open: mid-Mar–Jun & Sept daily 10am–4.30pm; Jul & Aug daily 10am–5pm. Admission charge.

Co Tyrone

The largest county in Northern Ireland, County Tyrone stretches southwest of enormous Lough Neagh. Near the lake shores are prehistoric stone circles and one of the finest high crosses in Ireland, while to the west beyond the peatlands lie the beautiful Sperrin Mountains.

Altmore Open Farm, Trout Fishery and Caravan Park

Visitors can learn about the history of the Sperrin Mountains region and see rare breeds of farm animals and poultry on this 71-hectare (175-acre) sheep farm. There is pony trekking in summer, and fishing.

32 Altmore Rd, 5km (3 miles) south of Pomeroy. Tel: (028) 8775 8977. Open: daily 9am–dusk. Admission charge.

Ardboe Cross

On the west shore of Lough Neagh is one of Ireland's finest northern high crosses, marking the site of a monastery. Over 5m (16ft) high, this 10th-century cross has scenes from the Old and New Testaments carved into it.

Off the B73, Lough Neagh, 16km (10 miles) east of Cookstown. Freely accessible.

Beaghmore Stone Circles

Beaghmore is a prehistoric site unique in Ireland. Discovered beneath a layer of peat, the origins and purpose of the seven Bronze Age stone circles and complex ceremonial area are unknown.

Signposted from the A505 between Cookstown & Gortin. Freely accessible.

Island Turf Craft and Bog Museum

Close to the peatlands, this privately owned museum is part of an outlet selling craft items carved from peat. The museum is filled with things found in the bog, such as extinct deer antlers.

Coalisland Enterprise Centre, 51 Dungannon Rd, Coalisland. Tel: (028) 8774 9041. www.island turfcrafts.com. Open: Mon–Sat 9am–5.30pm. Free admission.

Peatlands Park

This park tells the story of peat boglands over a period of 10,000 years.

There are areas of cutaway bogland, virgin bogs, small lakes and low wooded hills. A narrow-gauge railway, originally used for carrying turf, takes visitors out on to the bog.
Exit 13 from the M1, 11km (7 miles) east of Dungannon. Tel: (028) 3885 1102. Open: Easter–Sept daily 9am–9pm; Oct–Easter daily 9am–5pm. Visitor centre open: Easter–Sept daily 10am–6pm. Charge for railway.

President Grant's Ancestral Homestead
John Simpson, great-grandfather of Ulysses S Grant, 18th President of the United States, was born at Ballygawley in 1738 and emigrated to Pennsylvania in 1760. The two-room thatched farmhouse where he lived has been restored, and the adjoining visitor centre has an audiovisual theatre and exhibits of rural life.
Dergina, Ballygawley. Tel: (028) 8555 7133. Open: daily 9am–5pm. Free admission.

Ulster-American Folk Park
This open-air museum traces the connections of famous Americans with their Ulster ancestry, from Davy Crockett to an Archbishop of New York, including a handful of US presidents. The hard facts of 19th-century emigration are graphically demonstrated in the Ship and Dockside Gallery, where the smells and sounds of an overcrowded emigrant ship are reproduced.

2 Mellon Rd, Castletown, on the A5, 8km (5 miles) northwest of Omagh. Tel: (028) 8224 3292. www.folkpark.com. Open: Mar–Sept Tue–Sun 10am–5pm; Oct–Feb Tue–Fri 10am–4pm, Sat & Sun 11am–4pm. Last admission 90 mins before closing. Admission charge.

Wellbrook Beetling Mill
An 18th-century water-powered mill, restored to working order by the National Trust, demonstrates beetling – the final stage in the production of linen.
Off the A505, Corkhill, 6.5km (4 miles) west of Cookstown. Tel: (028) 8675 1735. www.nationaltrust.org.uk. Open: 12 Mar–21 Apr & Sept Sat & Sun 2–6pm; 22 Apr–1 May Fri–Tue 1–6pm; Jul–Aug Thur–Tue 2–6pm. Last admission 1 hr before closing. Admission charge.

Wilson Ancestral Home
This simple thatched, whitewashed house in the Sperrin Mountains was the home of the grandfather of the 28th US President, Woodrow Wilson. It still contains some of the original furniture.
Dergalt, 3km (2 miles) southeast of Strabane. Tel: (028) 7188 3735 for details. Open: Jul & Aug Tue–Sun 2–5pm or by arrangement. Guided tours only. Free admission.

Co Donegal
Ireland's third-largest county, Donegal covers the northwestern corner of the

island and feels very remote in places. Its rugged, rocky coastline, pristine hidden beaches, dramatic sea cliffs and Derryveagh Mountains make for some spectacular drives.

Donegal Castle

Close to the town centre, this fortified manor house dates from the 15th century, but underwent much rebuilding in the early 17th century, when it was incorporated into a Jacobean structure by Sir Basil Brooke.
Tirchonaill St, Donegal. Tel: (073) 22405. Open: Easter–mid-Sept daily 10am–6pm; rest of year Thur–Mon 9.30am–4.30pm. Last admission 45 mins before closing. Admission charge.

Donegal County Museum

Artefacts dating from the Stone Age to the 20th century are exhibited here.
High Rd, Letterkenny. Tel: (074) 912 4613. Open: Mon–Fri 10am–12.30pm & 1–4.30pm, Sat 1–4.30pm. Free admission.

Errigal Mountain

Errigal is Donegal's highest peak at 752m (2,467ft). Avid hikers say it is an

The beautifully maintained Donegal Castle

easy climb; others say scrabbling on the loose scree and the near-perpendicular topmost peak can be daunting. All agree that the view from the summit is supreme.
Dunlewey. Freely accessible.

Glebe Gallery

The Glebe Gallery houses the art collection of Derek Hill, landscape and portrait painter, who worked here until 1954. He presented the house and collection, which includes works by Picasso and Renoir, to the nation in 1981.
On the shores of Garton Lough, by Glenveagh Park. Tel: (074) 913 7071. Open: Easter week, Jul & Aug daily 11am–6.30pm; Jun & Sept Sat–Thur 11am–6.30pm. Last tour 1 hr before closing. Admission charge.

Glencolumbkille Folk Village Museum

The Folk Village features a group of three traditional-style cottages spanning three centuries, each furnished according to the period it represents (1700s, 1800s and 1900s).
Glencolumbkille. Tel: (074) 973 0017. www.glenfolkvillage.com. Open: Easter–Sept Mon–Sat 10am–6pm, Sun noon–6pm. Admission charge.

Glenveagh National Park and Museum

Glenveagh is set around Donegal's highest peaks, with Mount Errigal rising 752m (2,467ft). The visitor centre introduces the 16,000-hectare (39,537-acre) park's natural history –

Loose scree makes Errigal a challenging climb for some

moorland, lakes and woodland. The dramatically sited castle here is set in glorious gardens.

There are nature trails, and one of Ireland's last two herds of red deer lives in the park.

Church Hill, 24km (15 miles) northwest of Letterkenny. Tel: (074) 913 7090. www.glenveaghnationalpark.ie. Park open: Mar–Oct daily 10am–6pm; Nov–Feb daily 9am–5pm. Last admission 1 hr before closing. Closed: Good Friday & Christmas week. Free admission; charge for guided tours of castle & gardens.

Grianan of Ailigh

Ancient circular fort on a hill with spectacular views of the Inishowen Peninsula. It is a formidable structure with extensive restoration performed in the late 19th century.

Off the N13 between Letterkenny & Derry. Free admission.

Newmills Corn and Flax Mills

The corn and flax mills at Newmills have been in existence since the early 1800s, and were still being run as a business as

late as the 1980s. The mills have been restored and both waterwheels are in working order.

Newmills, Letterkenny. Tel: (074) 912 5155. Open: mid-Jun–late Sept daily 10am–6pm. Free admission.

Slieve League

Europe's highest cliff face is spectacular, especially in the light of the setting sun. The best view is from Bunglau Point.

Signposted road to Teelin from Carrick on the road between Glencolumbkille & Killybegs.

Co Londonderry

Whether you call it Londonderry or Derry, its original Irish name, the county's capital city has some of the best-preserved medieval walls in all of Europe. The coastline offers lovely views over Lough Foyle and the Atlantic.

Guildhall

Neo-Gothic building with the history of Derry in stained glass.

Guildhall Square, Derry. Tel: (028) 7137 7335. Open: Mon–Fri 9am–5pm. Free admission.

Mussenden Temple

An 18th-century folly rotunda based on the Temple of Vesta in Tivoli outside Rome. It is spectacularly located above one of the best beaches in Ireland which stretches for 10km (6 miles). It has two names – Benone Strand and Magilligan Strand.

Hezlett Farm, Sea Rd, Castlerock. Tel: (028) 2073 1582. Grounds open: during daylight hrs. Free admission.

Roe Valley Country Park

Ulster's first domestic hydroelectric power station, opened in 1896, is on show here, and much of its original equipment is preserved.

Off the B192, 1.5km (1 mile) south of Limavady. Tel: (028) 7772 2074. Visitor centre open: Easter–Sept daily 9am–6pm; Oct–Easter daily 9am–5pm. Free admission to centre & park.

St Columb's Cathedral

Scenes from the great Siege of Derry (1688–9) are depicted in stained glass. An audiovisual show outlines the cathedral's history.

Bishop St Within, Derry. Tel: (028) 7126 7313. www.stcolumbscathedral.org. Open: Mar–Oct Mon–Sat 9am–5pm; Nov–Feb Mon–Sat 9am–4pm. Closed winter 1–2pm. Donations welcomed.

Tower Museum

Multimedia displays portray Derry's history.

Union Hall Place, Derry. Tel: (028) 7137 2411. Open: Jul & Aug Mon–Sat 10am–5pm, Sun 11am–3pm; Sept Mon–Sat 10am–5pm; Oct–Jun Tue–Sat 10am–5pm. Admission charge.

Co Antrim

The road along the coast of County Antrim is one of the most dramatic scenic drives in Ireland. It leads past the lovely Antrim Glens inland to the Giant's Causeway, one of the world's most amazing natural formations, and on to the seaside resorts of Portrush and Portstewart.

Andrew Jackson Centre

The parents of the 7th US President emigrated from Carrickfergus in 1765. This 18th-century thatched cottage stands on the site of their original home. Displays and a video cover the background to the Ulster–American emigration.

Boneybefore, Carrickfergus. Tel: (028) 9336 6455. Open: by appointment only. Free admission.

Carrick-a-Rede Rope Bridge

Visitors can cross a bridge constructed by local fishermen from planks of wood and wire, which spans the distance between the mainland and Rathlin Island, a frightening 24m (79ft) above water.

Off the B15, 8km (5 miles) west of Ballycastle. Tel: (028) 2076 9839. www.nationaltrust.org.uk. Open: Mar–May, Sept & Oct daily 10am–6pm; Jun–Aug daily 10am–7pm; Nov–Feb daily 10.30am–3.30pm. Last entry to rope bridge 45 mins before closing. Admission charge. Visitor centre open: May weekends & public holidays; summer daily 1–5pm.

Carrickfergus Castle
Northern Ireland's largest, best-preserved Norman castle was begun by John de Courcy in 1180.
Marine Highway, Carrickfergus. Tel: (028) 9335 1273. Open: daily 10am–6pm. Last admission 30 mins before closing. Admission charge.

Dunluce Castle
The ruined cliff-top castle is a wonderfully eerie place that is said to be haunted by the spirits of its servants, who all perished when a raging storm blew the whole kitchen into the sea.
Near Bushmills. Tel: (028) 2073 1938. www.ehsni.gov.uk. Open: daily 10am–6pm. Admission charge.

Giant's Causeway
A World Heritage Site, the Causeway consists of 40,000 hexagonal basalt columns – an incredible freak of nature.

The natural formation of columns at Giant's Causeway almost appears man-made

The National Trust Visitor Centre has fascinating displays of the region's geology, flora and fauna and local history exhibits.
Port-na-Spaniagh, a short walk east of the Causeway, is the site of the wrecked Spanish Armada treasure ship *Girona*.
On the B146, Causeway Head, 3km (2 miles) north of Bushmills. Causeway freely accessible (a minibus with wheelchair access runs daily from the visitor centre). Visitor centre: tel: (028) 2073 1855. www.nationaltrust.org.uk. Open: Jul & Aug daily 9.30am–7pm; rest of year earlier closing. Admission charge for car park, the audiovisual show & minibus.

Lisburn Museum
Nice little exhibition on the process of turning flax into linen.
Market Square, Lisburn. Tel: (028) 9266 3377. Open: Mon–Sat 9.30am–5pm. Free admission.

Old Bushmills Distillery
Established in 1608, Bushmills is the world's oldest licensed distillery. Visitors are taken on a one-hour guided tour ending with a dram.
Distillery Rd, Bushmills. Tel: (028) 2073 3218 (ask for tours department). www.bushmills.com. Open: Apr–Oct Mon–Sat 9.15am–5pm, Sun noon–5pm (last tour 4pm); Nov–Mar Mon–Fri 9.15am–4.45pm, Sat & Sun 12.30–4.45pm (last tour 3.30pm). Tours only. Closed: 12 Jul. Admission charge.

Tour: Fermanagh lakeland

Fermanagh is an area of stunning beauty, with lakes and mountains, mysterious islands, and hints at a pagan past. It has a number of man-made attractions too, from Enniskillen Castle to the stately homes of Florence Court and Castle Coole.

Allow 1 day.

Begin at Enniskillen.

1 Enniskillen

Enniskillen straddles the River Erne. Watergate, part of the old castle, now houses the Fermanagh County Museum and the Regimental Museum. Oscar Wilde and Samuel Beckett were both old boys of Portora Royal School.

Take the A32 for 3km (2 miles), then the B82 for 11km (7 miles), turning off to Castle Archdale.

2 Castle Archdale

The estate has a butterfly park, an arboretum and rare breeds of farm animals. The ruins of an old castle, razed in 1689, can be seen in the forest.

White Island, with strange stone figures in a ruined church, can be reached by boat from Castle Archdale.

Turn left on the B82 and after 3km (2 miles) leave the B road and follow the scenic route for 6km (4 miles) to Kesh, then turn left on to the A35 for 1.5km (1 mile) before taking the A47 for 13km (8 miles) to Boa Island.

3 Boa Island

Towards the far end of the island, watch for a sign to Caldragh Graveyard on the left. Park by the road and walk for about 1km (²/₃ mile). At the end of the concrete track an old graveyard contains two stone figures: a double-faced Janus smiling on one side, scowling on the other, and a small hunched figure leering disconcertingly.

Continue on the A47 for 16km (10 miles).

4 Belleek

A border village, Belleek is famed for its fine basketwork china (*see p112*).

Take the A46 for Enniskillen, and, after 33km (21 miles), turn right and follow the signs to Monea.

5 Monea

Monea is a ruined 17th-century castle, built by 'planters' from Scotland. It was captured by the Irish in 1641 and abandoned in 1750. An ancient crannog – artificial island dwelling – can be traced in the marsh in front of Monea.

*Turn left leaving Monea, then right,
following signs for Boho for 8km
(5 miles). Turn right for Belcoo.*

6 Belcoo

Belcoo is noted for its coarse fishing.
To the north is the Holywell shrine.
*Cross into the Republic at Blacklion, then
back into Northern Ireland. Follow the
south shore of Lower Lough Macnean.
Turn right along Marlbank Scenic Loop
and drive for 5km (3 miles).*

7 Marble Arch Caves

Boats take visitors on a tour of this
spectacular underground system of
caverns (*see p114*). There is an excellent
visitor centre and beautiful countryside.
*Turn left, then right, and drive for 6km
(4 miles) to Florence Court.*

8 Florence Court

This grand Anglo-Irish mansion was
built in the early 18th century (*see p113*).
Return to Enniskillen by the A32 and A4.

Tour: Fermanagh lakeland

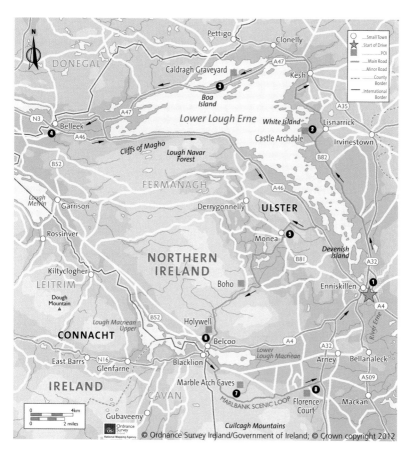

© Ordnance Survey Ireland/Government of Ireland; © Crown copyright 2012

Getting away from it all

Most people who know Ireland well will argue that simply being there is getting away from it all. Those seeking solitude may have to travel a little further than the rest, for the Irish are a gregarious people – but quiet places there are in abundance.

Beaches

There is no shortage of beaches along Ireland's shoreline. Many are as lovely as you will find anywhere in the world, ranging from long stretches of deserted dunes to intimate rocky coves.

There are beaches for all tastes and ages – lovely seasides with funfairs behind them, deserted white sands, roaring waves for surfers, fossil-strewn cliffs for collectors and calm quiet bays for swimmers. There are even beaches for car lovers, where they can drive their cars without bothering a soul.

Leinster

Close to Dublin, on the DART system, Dalkey and Killiney (pronounced 'Dorkee' and 'Kill-aye-nee') are attractive spots for a half-day's outing. Dalkey has narrow streets and elegant houses. Boat trips can be taken during the summer to Dalkey Island, which has a bird sanctuary and a Martello tower. Killiney, set in a sweeping bay with neat villas, lush gardens and the backdrop of the two Wicklow sugarloaf mountains, is often compared with the Bay of Naples.

Courtown, Co Wexford, is a pleasant harbour village 40km (25 miles) north of Wexford town. Its 3km (2-mile)-long sandy beach, amusements and golf course make it a popular family resort. Also in Co Wexford, Kilmore Quay, about 19km (12 miles) southwest of Rosslare, is a pretty fishing village with excellent beaches.

Munster

Ardmore, Co Waterford, is a charming resort with a good beach at the base of a cliff. About 21km (13 miles) southwest of Dungarvan, it has impressive monastic ruins surrounding an almost intact round tower. Birdwatchers will be attracted to Castlegregory, Co Kerry, on the western shore of Tralee Bay. The beaches are superb, and many unusual species – including Bewick's swans – have been logged at the nearby Lough Gill bird sanctuary.

Dunmore East, Co Waterford, is a delightful village of thatched cottages and friendly pubs overlooking a picturesque bay and fishing harbour 16km (10 miles) south of Waterford. Its sandy beaches are protected by rose-hued cliffs.

Lahinch is the busiest resort in Co Clare, but there is still plenty of room along its splendid beach and nearby dunes. The surfing is good and there is a championship golf course.

Connacht

Some 100km (62 miles) northwest of Galway City, Roundstone is a relaxing, pretty village resort on the edge of a bay and has become a popular summer destination. First settled by Scottish fishermen in the 19th century, today it has a community of artists and crafts folk whose workshops may be visited.

Spiddall, 19km (12 miles) west of Galway, has a well-named beach in the Silver Strand. There is good shore fishing, and in the summer there are exciting races between currachs, the traditional canvas-skinned boats. Just 8km (5 miles) west of Sligo, Strandhill is a favoured place for surfing championships. For those who prefer quieter waters, Culleenamore, round the corner in Ballysadare Bay, is the place.

Ulster

Standing on a beautiful beach on Lough Swilly, Rathmullen in Co Donegal has a ruined 16th-century priory and an informative heritage centre. It is also the start of the Fanad Drive, with even more wonderful beaches, as well as streams, lakes and mountains.

Cushendun, Co Antrim, was built in the style of a Cornish village – a tribute by Lord Cushendun to his Cornish wife. There is a good beach, and from nearby Torr Head you can see Scotland's Mull of Kintyre. Newcastle, Co Down, is where 'the Mountains of Mourne sweep down to the sea'. A traditional and popular resort, it has a magnificent sandy beach. Towering 852m (2,795ft) above the town is Slieve Donard.

Islands

Storm-battered or bathed in sunshine, obscured by mist or magnified in the strange light of a rainbow sky, the islands of Ireland beckon with a promise of rugged freedom.

Most of the islands lie within 8km (5 miles) of the mainland and none is more than 16km (10 miles) out. Each has been inhabited at some time – the wildest by no more than a hermit monk or two in the early days of Christianity. Celtic crosses, ruined chapels and dwellings are everywhere. A few are still inhabited and some have family-run hotels and guesthouses. Visit *www.irelandsislands.com* for information.

The north

Five kilometres (3 miles) off the coast of Donegal, **Aranmore Island** is served by a ferry from Burtonport (*tel: (074) 952 0532; www.arranmoreferry.com*). The island is hilly, with rough moorland and cliffs on the Atlantic side and sandy beaches and rock pools facing the mainland. Seven pubs and a hotel set the pace of the island's social life.

Rathlin, off the north coast of Co Antrim, is home to 30 families, mostly involved in raising sheep and cattle. Settled originally by early Christian monks, Rathlin has suffered plunder, piracy and massacre. The cave in which Robert the Bruce studied a resolute spider can be visited in good weather. The island has a bird sanctuary, a diving centre, three lighthouses, a couple of bed and breakfasts, and a pub. The crossing from Ballycastle takes about 50 minutes (*tel: (028) 2076 9299; www.rathlinballycastleferry.com*).

The west

The three **Aran Islands** – Inishmore, Inishmaan and Inisheer – dominate the

The ruins of Dún Aengus prehistoric fort perch on a cliff 90m (295ft) above the sea on Inishmore

Aran Islands
For ferries to the Aran Islands, *see pp185–6*. Flights depart from Indreabhan, 27km (17 miles) west of Galway City and reached by a shuttle bus from the city. *Tel: (091) 593034. www.aranislands.ie*

Clare Island
Ferry services operate from Roonagh Pier, near Louisburg (*tel: (098) 23737; www.clareislandferry.com* and *tel: (098) 25045; www.omalleyferries.com*). Both these companies run ferries throughout the year. Trips take 15 minutes.

Dursey Island
Cable car departs daily from Ballaghboy at the end of the Beara Peninsula. *Tel: (028) 21766.*

Cape Clear
See p186.

horizon off the coasts of Clare and Galway. Like The Burren, the islands consist mainly of bare, grey limestone scoured by ice-age glaciers. But the bleakness is tempered by stone-walled pastures and wild flowers.

Inishmore, the largest, has 14 small villages and a fishing harbour at Kilronan. Dún Aengus is the largest of several prehistoric forts and there are many early Christian churches, including the 7th-century St Benan's.

Inishmaan has two impressive prehistoric forts and the cottage in which the writer J M Synge lived.

Inisheer, southernmost of the islands, has narrow roads and a gleaming white beach on which currachs are built.

Rising to a height of some 500m (1,640ft) in Clew Bay, Co Mayo, **Clare Island** will appeal to walkers. It also offers fishing, sailboarding, pony trekking and diving. The island wildlife includes dolphins, seals and otters, and it is also home to the chough, a rare, red-billed crow. A square tower near the harbour was the stronghold of Grace O'Malley, the 16th-century pirate who declared herself queen of Clew Bay and held her own against Elizabeth I on a visit to London in 1575.

The southwest

A cable car links **Dursey Island** to the mainland off the tip of the Beara Peninsula in Co Cork. Popular with birdwatchers, who climb the western cliffs to observe gannets and search for rare migrants, the island has no paved roads. Transport is not necessary on Dursey and you can walk wherever you like.

Cape Clear, Ireland's southernmost island, challenges the Atlantic from Roaringwater Bay in West Cork. About 5km (3 miles) long, the island is wild and precipitous, but there are tiny pastures and its houses are protected by hedges of fuchsia and escallonia. During the summer its population of 150 is swollen by the visitors, naturalists and Irish-language students who travel by ferries from Schull and Baltimore.

Waterways

You don't have to drive very far in Ireland before encountering a lough (lake) or river. But why drive? Both the Republic and Northern Ireland offer alternatives in the form of waterway holidays. Vital in the days before the railways, the waterways have become a rich legacy of leisure, affording a relaxing opportunity to gain a backyard view of Ireland at its best.

The Republic has three major waterway systems, each connected to the other. From Dublin, the Grand Canal runs westwards to meet the stately River Shannon. Less than halfway along its route, a branch of the canal goes off to meet the River Barrow, which provides a navigable route south to St Mullins before reaching the sea at Waterford.

Northern Ireland has Lough Erne – Upper and Lower – a superb lakeland cruising area, with an island, they'll tell you, for every day of the year.

Thanks to restoration work on a derelict canal, the Shannon–Erne Waterway now connects the River Shannon with Lough Erne, enabling

Grand Canal
Barrowline Cruisers (*Vicarstown, Co Laois; tel: (057) 862 6060; www.barrowline.ie*) offers English-style narrowboats for hire.
River Shannon
Ten companies offer nearly 400 self-skippered boats for hire on the Shannon. Details in *Ireland's Magic Waterways* available from Bord Fáilte offices (*see p188*).
River Barrow
Barowline Cruisers – *see* Grand Canal *above.*
Lough Erne
Fermanagh Tourist Information Centre, *Wellington Rd, Enniskillen, Co Fermanagh. Tel: (028) 6632 3110.*

The Irish countryside is green and inviting and water is never very far away

boaters to cruise freely over some 800km (497 miles) between the provinces of Leinster, Munster and Ulster.

The Grand Canal

Between Lucan, just outside Dublin, and Shannon Harbour, there are only 36 locks in a distance of about 130km (81 miles). Robertstown, where the River Barrow link starts, is an attractive village with a boating centre and a base for hiring cruisers. Edenderry, on a spur off the canal's main line, has excellent moorings in a pretty harbour. Tullamore is the home of *Tullamore Dew* whiskey and the liqueur Irish Mist. Shannon Harbour, marking the entrance to Ireland's major river, was once a thriving inland port. It now provides a safe haven for many boaters.

River Shannon

The Shannon contains the largest area of inland water in Britain and Ireland. It flows southwards for 350km (217 miles), following a course rich in history between Co Cavan, where it rises, and the Atlantic Ocean. It passes through only one city – Limerick – but it provides an opportunity to view and visit some of Ireland's finest historic sites, including the stunning Clonmacnoise (*see p56*), the most important early Christian monastic settlement. Carrick-on-Shannon, a popular starting point for cruising holidays, has some fine Georgian buildings.

Along its length, the Shannon has a wealth of birdlife and flora and it is flanked by ancient woodlands. There are nature trails to explore at Portumna Castle, on the shore of Lough Derg and in Lough Key Forest Park.

River Barrow

The river passes through many fascinating places. Athy is a market town whose history goes back to medieval times. Carlow has a Norman castle. Graiguenamanagh is a photogenic town with the restored Duiske Abbey, founded in 1207. St Mullins, near the end of the navigation, has associations with early Celtic mythology.

Lough Erne

Cruising offers the best way to see many of Fermanagh's attractions. Mooring up at Devenish and White Islands, for example, enables you to view their mysterious ruins and relics without the crowds. Devenish is wonderful by moonlight (*see p113*). Navigation throughout the Erne system is easy and boating facilities are excellent.

Hiking and cycling

Great country for walking and cycling, in mountain, forest, glen and valley, can be found throughout Ireland. The **Ulster Way**, an 800km (497-mile) circular footpath, follows the Northern Ireland coastline, returning to Belfast through the Sperrin Mountains, the Fermanagh Lakeland and the Mountains of Mourne.

In the Republic there are 27 marked long-distance walking routes. At 35km (22 miles), the Burren Way is the shortest (but one of the most beautiful), and the Wicklow Way, at 132km (82 miles), is one of the oldest of the waymarked walks and covers some beautiful scenery. The most stunning of the waymarked routes are considered to be in the southwest of Ireland: the Kerry Way (210km/130 miles) is an eight-day walk that winds its way around the Iveragh Peninsula, making use of old butter roads and climbing through some of the most unspoilt countryside in Ireland. Several tour companies organise luggage transfers from one stage of the walk to the next. The Sheep's Head Way (88km/55 miles) travels the tiny and rarely visited Sheep's Head Peninsula, finding routes along mountain ridges and along the cliffs of the northern shore.

Most of Ireland's roads, being relatively free of motor traffic, are fairly safe for careful cyclists, and many areas are ideal for all-terrain bikes, which can be hired in the north and south. Specialists who arrange walking and cycling holidays, with or without a guide, are listed on Fáilte Ireland's website (*www.discoverireland.ie*). You can also try *www.cycleni.com*

INFORMATION

National Waymarked Ways Irish Sports Council, *Westend Office Park, Blanchardstown, Dublin 15. Tel: (01) 860 8800.*
www.irishtrails.ie
Ulster Way Countryside Access and Activities Network, *The Stableyard, Barnett's Demesne, Malone Rd, Belfast. Tel: (028) 9030 3930.*
www.walkni.com/ulsterway
Cycling Ireland *Kelly Roche House, 619 North Circular Rd, Dublin 1. Tel: (01) 855 1522.*
www.cyclingireland.ie

Shopping

Many of the souvenirs on sale to visitors are bought at shops within craft centres, factories and mills, after they have seen the goods at various stages of production. Some of these shops stock a range of products made elsewhere in Ireland. Good-quality mementos and gifts are also on sale at tourist offices.

Both Dublin and Belfast have compact city centres. Both cities have some splendid multi-storey, covered shopping centres – among them Westbury Mall and the Powerscourt Town House Centre in Dublin and Castle Court in Belfast.

In Dublin, pedestrianised Grafton Street and its environs and wide O'Connell Street are the main places for the committed shopper, with windows displaying classic clothes and exciting new styles and designer knitwear. Nearby Nassau Street has a parade of shops, some of which are still in the hands of the families that founded them. Exquisite woollens and tweeds are on sale. One shop sells men's and women's suits, jackets and hats in hand-woven Donegal tweed, and lengths of tweed can be bought, so that customers can have them made up when they get home.

Large American-style malls are becoming increasingly popular – Dundrum in the suburbs of Dublin has the largest one in Ireland.

Belfast's waterfront redevelopment scheme includes some upmarket shops within a conference centre, concert hall and hotel complex.

Belfast is the traditional home of Irish linen and this can be found in several of the city's arcades and pedestrianised-area shops. Handmade woollens, pottery and glassware are welcome gifts. The Space CRAFT shop in the Fountain Centre sells a wide range of locally made crafts, while the Smithfield Market offers a number of small specialised shops under one roof.

Cork City shops are mostly small and interesting, each retailer an expert in his or her field. High-quality fashions are elegantly displayed cheek by jowl with bookshops, tobacconists, pharmacies, hardware stores, toy shops and jewellers. Crescent-shaped St Patrick's Street is the main shopping thoroughfare and a pedestrianised area is flanked by Carey's Lane, French Church Street and Paul Street.

Galway's Church Lane Market (*Sat & public holidays 8am–6pm, Sun 2–6pm*) has stalls selling all manner of craft items.

Waterford City presents itself as the 'Shopping Capital of the Southeast' and is indeed a vibrant centre with a range of specialist outlets lining its narrow streets. The city is particularly good for local, hand-crafted pottery, textiles and jewellery. Visit *www.waterfordtourism.org*

Pottery, already firmly established in some areas – Belleek is the best known (*see p112*) – is a developing craft, and pottery studios are opening up all over.

You can still see handmade Irish harps, made in Mayo, Meath and Dublin.

Craftspeople in Limerick, Clare and Cork make chairs and stools in local ash or beech. Burnished blackthorn is used for walking sticks. Good examples of the blacksmith's craft are produced in Cork and Kerry.

Jewellery in silver, gold and enamel is created in unusual and classic designs. The famous Claddagh ring – the lovers' symbol of two hands cradling a crowned heart – can be found exquisitely crafted in sterling silver.

Basket weaving and rushwork are homecrafts producing a variety of goods, including table mats. Among other crafts practised around the country are batik work – fairly new to Ireland – stained glass, tapestry, fly-tying and leatherwork.

A three-week Shopping Spree takes place in Sligo each autumn, with bargains to be had all over town.

Throughout the country many of the shops selling crafts and goods of Irish manufacture run a mailing service.

Visitors from outside the European Union are entitled to reclaim the cost of Value Added Tax (VAT) on purchases made in the Republic and Northern Ireland.

Dublin's pedestrianised Grafton Street

WHERE TO SHOP

Tucked away all over rural Ireland are craft workshops, potteries, weavers, woodcarvers and jewellers, some long established and others young and inventive, and all of them with an eye to the new economic realities. Before you leave Dublin, visit the big shops around Nassau St and Dawson St to get a picture of what is available around the country and then, as you travel, check out the workshops themselves. You might get better bargains, seconds or just the pleasure of watching the things being made.

Antiques
Co Cork
Linda's This shop specialises in antique jewellery, but also has collections of books, paintings and other knick-knacks.
Main St, Kinsale.
Tel: (021) 774754.

Co Donegal
The Gallery Paintings, antiques, crafts.
Dunfanaghy.
Tel: (074) 913 6224.
Mourne Antiques A great place to browse for Irish collectibles, china, jewellery and antique furniture. If you change your mind when you get home and decide you want something, you can visit their website and have it sent to you.
8 Port Rd, Letterkenny.
Tel: (074) 912 6457.
www.mourneantiques.com

Co Dublin
Blackrock Market *19a Main St, Blackrock.*
Tel: (01) 283 3522. www.blackrockmarket.com.
Open: Sat 11am–5.30pm, Sun noon–5.30pm.

Art
Co Galway
The Kenny Gallery Long-established art gallery and bookshop, this place has recently relocated to a retail park in the outskirts of town but is well worth the journey. The gallery hosts exhibitions of paintings, sculpture and more by well-known and upcoming Irish and European artists.
Liosbán Retail Park, Tuam Rd, Galway.
Tel: (091) 709350.
www.thekennygallery.ie

Co Kerry
Killarney Art Gallery (Mulvany Bros) The work of Irish painters is on sale here.
5 Plunkett St, Killarney.
Tel: (064) 34628.
www.irishartcollector.com

Books
Co Dublin
Easons *40 O'Connell St, Dublin 1.*
Tel: (01) 858 3800.
Hodges Figgis *56–58 Dawson St, Dublin 2.*
Tel: (01) 677 4754.

Crafts
Belfast
Conway Mill Craft Centre Traditional Irish crafts, linens, textiles and jewellery.
Conway Mill, Conway St.
Tel: (028) 9032 6452.

Co Cork
Blarney Woollen Mills Selection of Irish goods.
Blarney. Tel: (021) 438 5280. www.blarney.com.

Also in Bunratty, Galway, Killarney and Tipperary.

Kinsale Crystal Small, family-run crystal workshop and store selling hand-cut crystal. Watch the craftspeople at work, select your own crystalware and have it delivered.
Market St, Kinsale.
Tel: (021) 477 4493.
www.kinsalecrystal.ie

Trag Knitwear Selection of hand- and machine-knit Aran sweaters. Fashions, crafts. Bargain basement.
Tragumna, Skibbereen.
Tel: (028) 21750.

Co Donegal
Magee Established 1866. Magee's hand-woven tweed is still made in cottages and finished in the factory.
The Diamond, Donegal.
Tel: (074) 972 2660.
www.mageedonegal.com

Triona Fashions Factory shop. Ladies' fashions in tweed as well as Irish handknits.
Ardara.
Tel: (074) 954 1422.

Co Dublin
Avoca Handweavers Upmarket fashion, toys and gifts.
11–13 Suffolk St, Dublin.
Tel: (01) 672 6019.
www.avoca.ie

Designyard Four floors of jewellery, art pieces and sculpture.
48–49 Nassau St, Dublin 2.
Tel: (01) 474 1011.
www.designyard.ie

The Kilkenny Shop 6 *Nassau St, Dublin 2.*
Tel: (01) 677 7066.
www.kilkennyshop.com

Co Kerry
Quill's Woollen Market Claims the best selection of designer handknits and woollen goods. Also in Sneem and Kenmare.
Market Cross, Killarney.
Tel: (064) 32277.

Co Kilkenny
Kilkenny Design Centre Showcases Irish crafts and has a wide range of handcrafted gifts and fashion items.
Castle Yard, Kilkenny.
Tel: (056) 772 2118.
www.kilkennydesign.com

Jewellery
Belfast
The Steensons Ltd Northern Ireland's leading designer jewellery store. Visit the workshop and showroom in the village of Glenarm on weekdays to see pieces being made.
Bedford House, Bedford St.
Tel: (028) 9024 8269.
www.thesteensons.com

Co Cork
Victoria's Pretty collection of antique and reproduction jewellery.
2 Oliver Plunkett St, Cork. Tel: (021) 427 2752.

Co Sligo
The Cat & The Moon Handcrafted silver and gold. Work by other Irish artists.
4 Castle St, Sligo.
Tel: (071) 914 3686. www. thecatandthemoon.com

WF Henry Large range of jewellery and watches, including Claddagh rings in gold and silver.
2 High St, Sligo.
Tel: (071) 914 2658.

Textile crafts

Creating textiles for Avoca's wool mills on a several-hundred-year-old loom

Crafts usually develop where the raw materials are available. It follows, therefore, that homespun tweeds and woollens were traditionally based in noted sheep-rearing areas like Donegal, Galway, Kerry, Mayo and Wicklow. Each region had its distinctive product, depending not only on the local wool used, but also on the local dyes.

In parts of Donegal, long famous for its strong tweed, hand-weaving continues as a cottage industry. The crafts of hand knitting and hand embroidery are also still found here. In the same areas, workshops can be visited where a new generation of weavers produces lighter, brighter textiles – scarves, dress lengths, rugs and wall hangings.

Aran sweaters are never out of fashion, though they owe their origin to the fact that they are practical – thick, warm and rain-resistant – and ideal for wintry weather. Even the intricate patterns devised by families and passed down from one generation to the next were rooted in practicality, if a somewhat morbid one. It is said they were a means of identifying drowned fishermen.

Irish hand crochet work is a much-sought-after fashion accessory today.

Weaving linen is now limited to Northern Ireland. A little flax is still grown there, but most is imported. Beetling – hammering the cloth to produce a smooth sheen – is the final process in linen manufacturing. Wellbrook Beetling Mill, near Cookstown, Co Tyrone, opens for spring and summer afternoons and is well worth a visit (*see p115*).

The **Middle House Museum**, at Upperlands, Maghera, Co Londonderry, has a private textile museum opened by appointment by the Clark family, who live there. The machinery dates from 1740 (*tel: (028) 7954 7210* to arrange a guided tour).

Yarn was bleached by boiling and laid out to dry on 'bleach greens'. Northern Ireland had about 360 bleach greens in the industry's late 18th-century heyday.

Many textiles are produced using the time-honoured traditional ways

Entertainment

Ireland does not immediately spring to mind when planning a holiday with a sizzling nightlife, but you would be wrong to dismiss it altogether. Much of the nightlife is impromptu. A lot of it takes place in pubs and bars; places where people know they can relax over a drink in pleasant company, and where there is always a chance of someone striking up a tune on a tin whistle, a guitar or fiddle, or even the uilleann *pipes. And suddenly there's a singsong, a* seisiun *or 'session', as they call it.*

This is the *craic*, the good-time fun factor, and if you don't want strong drink you can get it with tea or coffee. To go to Ireland and not visit the bars is as unthinkable as going to Egypt without seeing the pyramids. The smoking ban has changed their atmosphere for the better, with most bars finding some space outside for what can very loosely be called a 'beer garden', where those in need of a fix can huddle around outdoor gas heaters.

All towns of any size can offer cinemas, live music of all descriptions,

Rosie O'Grady's is a well-known name

clubs for the young and nightowl-ish, and the occasional amateur or travelling theatre production, while most villages gear up for the tourists with festivals celebrating everything from oysters to literature. There are circus tours during the summer in the smaller towns, horse trotting and racing in the streets, and on a good night spontaneous poetry recitals, Irish music or wicked card games in the bars.

Cork, Galway, Sligo and Limerick all have tourist-oriented entertainment from theatre to *Riverdance*-like shows. In Dublin, big names visit venues like the Point and the Helix. There are film and theatre festivals during the summer, blockbuster and arthouse cinemas, too many clubs for you to take in during a single visit to the city, and pubs on every corner catering to every age group, bank balance, sexual orientation and ability to tolerate loud music. If you are into Irish dance and folk music you can spend a whole evening eating, drinking, watching and taking part in the whole shebang – set dancing, oysters in beer, Irish stew and fiddle music, all in the one, slightly cheesy, possibly even thatched, bar. Lots of bars have comedy nights and there is a dedicated comedy venue in the city centre. History buffs will love walking tours of the city, and sports fans can join the crowds at the many sporting venues.

To find out what is on, keep an eye on the local newspapers. For more detailed news of what to see and do, call at the tourist information office. Apart from leaflets on local attractions and festivals, free newspapers and free magazines, such as *What About* for Belfast or the online Event Guide for Dublin (*www.dublineventguide.com*), are a mine of information.

Entire regions, like the northwest (Cavan, Donegal, Leitrim, Monaghan and Sligo) and Shannon (Clare, Limerick, North Kerry, North Tipperary and South Offaly), are covered in annual visitors' guides and on websites. Many small towns have a privately published freesheet, like the *Tralee Advertiser.*

In Northern Ireland, the 20-page *Lakeland Extra* is distributed to homes and businesses in Fermanagh and South Tyrone and can also be picked up at various locations, including tourist information centres.

Most tourist boards have their own websites with 'What's On' sections or a local entertainment guide. Dublin's own tourist board site is

Fireworks over the Liffey

at *www.visitdublin.com*, and the official tourist board pages are at *www.discoverireland.com.* For arts and entertainment listings for Northern Ireland, see *www. culturenorthernireland.org*

The advice given in one of the free monthly papers for visitors is: 'Rest well to prepare for another day of fun and adventure in the region that nature has indeed given more than its fair share.' And why should anyone argue with that?

The Irish are a friendly, welcoming people. Nobody who seeks company is allowed to be lonely in Ireland. It is not that they are curious about you. They are not nosy. They do not intrude. They just recognise you are someone to talk to and the talk is never trite or tedious. It is straight from the heart, it is anecdotal, informative, showing interest in your responses, your impressions of Ireland and the Irish. It leads to humour, wit and laughter, it extends to others in your proximity and suddenly you are enjoying yourself.

WHAT'S ON

Many entertainments listed here take place only during the summer, and others, like live music in pubs, are limited to fewer appearances. Always check beforehand.

Amusement centres

See p144.

Banquets and hooleys

Co Clare

For all of the venues below, *tel: (061) 360788* or visit *www.shannon heritage.com/BookNow* for reservations.

Bunratty Castle Twice-nightly medieval banquet offered all year round. *Bunratty.*

Bunratty Folk Park Traditional Irish Night Irish stew and traditional Irish singing and dancing. *Bunratty. Nightly on demand. Book in advance.*

Knappogue Castle Nightly medieval banquets with musical entertainment from April to October. *Quin.*

Co Dublin

Abbey Tavern

Traditional Irish meal, followed by music and dancing in an old pub. This place gets booked up every night and the show has been running for decades. A whole night's entertainment, and you don't get turned out for the second sitting

like in the bigger places. *28 Abbey St, Howth. Tel: (01) 839 0307. www.abbeytavern.ie*

Johnny Fox's Pub Pure kitsch, but good fun: a meal, Irish music and dancing from 7.30pm until midnight in a genuinely ancient pub. Advance booking essential, no children after 7.30pm. *Glencullen. Tel: (01) 295 5647. www.jfp.ie*

Co Galway

Dunguaire Castle medieval banquet Extracts from works of Synge, Yeats and Gogarty. *Kinvara. www.shannon heritage.com. Apr–Oct 5.30pm & 8.45pm.*

Bowling

Co Limerick

Fun World Family Entertainment Centre Ten computerised lanes. *Ennis Rd, Limerick. Tel: (061) 325088. www.funworld.ie*

Comedy clubs

Co Cork

City Limits Comedy Club Bar and club; small venue, good atmosphere.

Pubs and bars are the focus of social life and evening entertainment

Coburg St, Cork.
Tel: (021) 450 1206.
www.thecomedyclub.ie.
Shows: Fri & Sat nights.

Co Dublin
**The International
Comedy Club** Long-
standing alternative
comedy venue, now six
nights a week and twice
on Saturdays. Good
value for money in a
lovely old
unreconstructed pub
where comedians such
as John Bishop, Ardal
O'Hanlon, Kevin Bridges
and Eddie Izzard have all
appeared.
23 Wicklow St, Dublin 2.
Tel: (01) 677 9250. www.
theinternationalcomedy
club.com. Open: times
vary, so check for details.
Laughter Lounge The
original Laughter
Lounge in Dublin has
been in business since
1997 and since then has
hosted over 3,000
comedians including
such famous names as
Ardal O'Hanlon, Jo
Brand, Dylan Moran, Bill
Bailey, Rich Hall, Jimmy
Carr, Paul Merton, Tony
Slattery, Dara O'Brian
and Michael McIntyre.

Basement, 4–8 Eden
Quay, O'Connell Bridge,
Dublin. Tel: (01) 878
3003. www.laughter
lounge.com. Shows usually
Thur–Sat 8.30pm (doors
open 7pm).

Concerts and opera
Belfast
Grand Opera House
See pp100–101.
**Queens University
School of Music**
Admission charge for
evening concerts.
University Square/
Botanic Ave.
Tel: (028) 9097 5337.
www.music.qub.ac.uk.
Free lunchtime recitals
autumn/winter.

Co Cork
Cork Opera House Irish
plays predominate in
summer. Opera, ballet,
musical comedy.
Emmet Place, Cork.
Tel: (021) 427 0022.
www.corkoperahouse.ie

Co Dublin
National Concert Hall
Leading venue for
classical music.
Earlsfort Terrace,
Dublin 2. Tel: (01) 417
0077. www.nch.ie

Co Londonderry
Guildhall Concerts
and dramatic
productions.
Shipquay St, Derry.
Tel: (028) 7137 7355.
www.derrycity.gov.uk/
guildhall

Nightclubs
Belfast
La Lea Premier spot
for dancing; until
3am.
43 Franklin St.
Tel: (028) 9023 0200.
Limelight
Disco/nightclub.
17 Ormeau Ave.
Tel: (028) 9032 5968.
Open: Tue, Fri & Sat.

Co Cork
An Seanachai Live
traditional music nightly
in summer and a club
upstairs.
Market St, Kinsale.
Tel: (021) 477 7077.

Co Dublin
Lillie's Bordello
Established nightclub
with trendy clientele.
Adam Court, Grafton St,
Dublin 2.
Tel: (01) 679 9204.
www.lilliesbordello.ie
(Cont. on p140)

The pubs

People rave about Ireland's pubs and bars – the *craic* or 'crack' (conversation and good-time factor), the character, the generally easy-going ambience. And justifiably. That is not to say, however, that some of them don't have dismal décor, plastic upholstery and archaic fittings. The trouble is, most have frosted windows or are heavily curtained, so you can't tell what they're like until you go in. However, at least three times out of four you'll be successful, and even the dreary ones usually have friendly staff and customers.

The traditional snug areas are still a feature of many old pubs – closed-in sections where a few friends can get together in relative privacy. There are plenty about. Blake's of

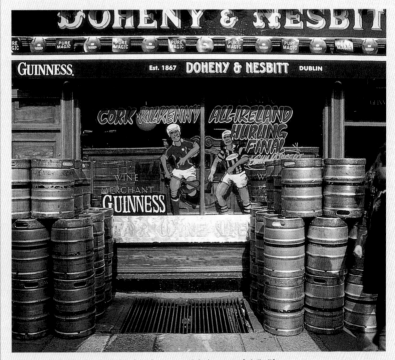

Pubs are an institution in Ireland and an essential element of daily life

Traditional music adds to the *craic*

the Hollow, 6 Church Street, in Enniskillen, is one. In Dublin's Lower Baggot Street there's Doheny and Nesbitt's. Another is Kehoe's, in South Anne Street, Dublin, whose snugs were immortalised by Sean O'Casey.

The Crown Liquor Saloon in Great Victoria Street, Belfast, is the city's most flamboyant. It was renovated in 1885 by an architect who was inspired by what he had seen in Spain and Italy. The result is red and yellow ceilings, a marble-topped bar with wooden arches and columns and panelled snugs with ornate carvings over the doors. The pub is cared for by

the National Trust, whose restoration work includes gas lamps (*see p103*).

Some Irish pubs have a theme. Platform of Holywood, Co Down, near the Belfast–Bangor railway, serves food and drink in what resembles railway carriages.

Music is a big attraction in many pubs – dozens of them in Dublin. Concerts are given at Purty Kitchen (*www.purtykitchen.com*) in Essex Street East, where traditional and folk, country and jazz are also played. Many world-famous singers and bands started as pub musicians in Ireland.

Co Londonderry
Sugar Nightclub Young people's rendezvous.
33 Shipquay St, Derry.
Tel: (028) 7126 6017.
Open: Wed & Fri–Sun.

Pub entertainment
Belfast
The John Hewitt Owned by the Belfast Unemployed Resource Centre, this pleasant pub in what was once a run-down area of the city has live music of some kind every night, and, best of all, no TV.
51 Donegall St, Belfast.
Tel: (028) 9023 3768.
www.thejohnhewitt.com
Kelly's Cellars Live music nightly. Saturday afternoon features folk, and Saturday night is blues.
30 Bank St, Belfast 1.
Tel: (028) 9024 6058.

Co Clare
O'Connor's One of Ireland's most famous pubs for live traditional music. If O'Connor's is full, try one of the other pubs – there's music pouring out of the woodwork in this cute little village.

Fisher St, Doolin.
Tel: (065) 707 4168.

Co Donegal
Shamrock Lodge Traditional Irish music, Saturday, July and August.
Falcarragh.
Tel: (074) 913 5057.

Co Dublin
Cobblestone Teetering on the verge of destruction, this fine old pub stands amid the ruins of the surrounding buildings, saved by the demise of the Celtic Tiger. Music every night in the bar, plus visiting bands in the room upstairs. There's a monthly spoken-word evening of storytelling, hip hop and poetry.
North King St, Dublin.
Tel: (01) 872 1799. www.
cobblestonepub.ie
O'Shea's Merchant Enormous pub, popular with office workers at lunchtime, and traditional music and dance lovers at night.
Lower Bridge St, Dublin.
Tel: (01) 679 3797.
www.osheashotel.com
The Temple Bar Big, red, crowded and always filled

with Irish music. The nights have a party atmosphere.
47–48 Temple Bar, Dublin.
Tel: (01) 672 5286/7.
www.thetemplebarpub dublin.com
Whelans A top live music venue.
25 Wexford St, Dublin 2.
Tel: (01) 478 0766.
www.whelanslive.com

Co Galway
Roísín Dubh Galway's premier music venue, this pub features a wide variety of live acts.
Dominick St.
Tel: (091) 586540.
www.roisindubh.net

Co Kerry
Danny Mann Inn Huge, gloriously loud, with traditional music.
Eviston House Hotel, Killarney. Apr–Dec daily; Dec–Mar Sat–Sun.
Séan Óg's Friendly pub with B&B, traditional Irish music.
41 Bridge St, Tralee.
Tel: (066) 712 8822.
www.sean-ogs.com.
Music Tue–Fri 9.30pm, Sat 10.30pm.

Co Limerick
Nancy Blake's
Traditional music
Monday, Wednesday and
Saturday.
Denmark St, Limerick.
Tel: (061) 416443.

Co Londonderry
Dungloe Bar One of the
town's best for music
and quizzes.
Waterloo St, Derry.
Tel: (028) 7126 7716.
www.thedungloebar.com

Co Sligo
Furey's Also known
as Sheela-na-gig, this
pub has live traditional
and regular music
weekends and some
weeknights. Monday is
open-mike.

Bridge St, Sligo.
Tel: (071) 43825.

Theatres
Belfast
Grand Opera House
Plays, opera and ballet.
2–4 Great Victoria St,
Belfast 1. Tel: (028) 9024
1919. www.goh.co.uk

Co Cork
Cork Opera House
Touring groups perform.
Booking office at Emmett
Place, Cork.
Tel: (021) 427 0022.
www.corkoperahouse.ie

Co Dublin
Abbey Theatre
Lower Abbey St, Dublin 1.
Tel: (01) 878 7222.
www.abbeytheatre.ie

Gate Theatre
Contemporary plays,
historic building.
1 Cavendish Row,
Parnell Square, Dublin 1.
Tel: (01) 874 4045.
www.gatetheatre.ie
Olympia Theatre
Comedy, dance, drama.
72 Dame St, Dublin 2.
Tel: (01) 679 3323.
www.olympia.ie

Co Galway
Town Hall Theatre
There's always something
on at the Town Hall
Theatre (or at the nearby
purpose-built Black Box
Theatre), whether it be
theatre, music or film.
Courthouse Square,
Galway. Tel: (091)
569777. www.tht.ie

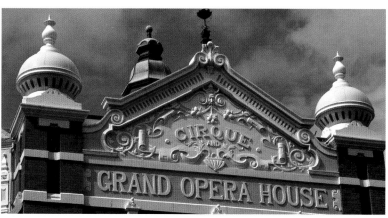

The façade of Belfast's Grand Opera House

Music, music, music!

You know it when you hear it – you can't stop your feet tapping. Traditional Irish music is difficult to define, but easy to enjoy.

Although each new Irish generation promotes its own interpretation of traditional music, and adds to the range of ballads, there has been a swell in the trend in recent years.

Notes of political strife, emigration and rebellion against authority creep into ballads. Overtones of bawdiness and lust have never been far away, and the sad solos of unrequited love, lost love and thwarted love continue to sell in mega-figures.

Irish singers and performers and Irish groups have worldwide impact. Music reverberates in the pubs and in the streets. Sometimes it is impromptu. Often it is 'all join in'.

The harp – the instrument most readily associated with Ireland – is still played as a traditional instrument today, and a musician playing one in Dublin's Grafton Street attracts huge crowds. The fiddle is at the hub of traditional Irish music.

The *uilleann* pipes, with the elbow used to pump air, are a refined version of bagpipes, and the *bodhrán* – a small goatskin drum – is popular

In a pub or out in the street, any time is a good time for music

The Oliver St John Gogarty pub in Dublin is famous for traditional music

in West Cork and Kerry. It is beaten with the knuckles or a soft, double-ended drumstick.

The tin whistle provides a merry accompaniment to other instruments, and the accordion and flute are often played solo.

The Republic has a central organisation for promoting music, song and dance – the Comhaltas. Its annual booklet, a guide to traditional music organised by Comhaltas branches nationwide, is available at no charge from tourist information centres. At the end of August the three-day All-Ireland Fleadh Cheoil na hÉireann, held in a different location each year, marks the highlight of the traditional music calendar.

IRELAND'S MUSICAL CALENDAR

Mar Arklow Music Festival
Apr & May Cork International Choral Festival
May Dublin International Piano Competition; Fleadh Nua Eims, Co Clare; Feis na nGleann, Ballycastle, Co Antrim
Jun KBC Music Festival – throughout Ireland; Belleek and Mulleek Traditional Music Festival, Belleek, Co Fermanagh
Jun & Jul West Cork Chamber Music Festival, Bantry, Co Cork
Jul Waltons Guitar Festival of Ireland, Dublin; Summer Music on the Shannon, Limerick
Jul & Aug O'Carolan Harp and Traditional Music Festival, Keadue, Co Roscommon; Ballyshannon Festival, Co Donegal
Sept Harvest Blues Festival, Co Monaghan; Johnny Keenan Banjo Festival, Co Longford
Oct Guinness Cork Jazz Festival; Wexford Opera Festival
Nov Spirit of Voice Festival, Galway

Children

Given good weather – and that is something that cannot be taken for granted in Ireland – many children are happy to spend time paddling in the sea and building sandcastles on the lovely and often uncrowded beaches. But the time comes when they want a little more adventure and excitement.

Amusement centres

Leisureland Amusement Park
Wide selection of rides, water slides and a heated indoor pool. Outside is an amusement park and minigolf.
Salthill, Co Galway. Tel: (091) 521455.
www.leisureland.ie

Tramore Amusement Park
Many rides and attractions. Tramore seafront also has a miniature railway.
Seafront, Tramore, Co Waterford.
Tel: (051) 391455.

Tropicana
Outdoor heated leisure pool with huge slide and smaller pool for infants.
Central Promenade, Newcastle,
Co Down. Tel: (028) 4372 5034.
Open: Jul & Aug.

Waterworld Bundoran
Flume ride, enormous slides, a pool for children and a seaweed bath for adults.
Bundoran. Tel: (071) 984 1172.
www.waterworldbundoran.com

Waterworld Portrush
An indoor complex with an 80m (262ft) water flume, whirlpools, water cannon and pirate ship, and relaxing saunas and steam rooms.
Portrush, Co Antrim.
Tel: (028) 7082 2001.

Beaches

Visitors to Ireland are spoilt for choice when it comes to Blue Flag, white-sand, empty beaches. In the North, **Portrush** in Co Antrim has donkey rides, Curran Strand and the arches and caves of the White Rocks, while **Portstewart Strand** is well known among surfers.

Bundoran in Co Donegal is a typical seaside town with huge areas of beach. On **Achill Island** are beautiful, deserted beaches stretching for many kilometres. In Co Galway, near Roundstone, are Gurteen Bay, Dogs Bay and Ballyconneely beach.

In the south and west, the **Dingle Peninsula** has vast empty beaches. **Barley Cove** on the Mizen Peninsula has large stretches of sand, a stream across the beach, dunes, and lifeguards on duty. Close by is an indoor pool.

The east coast has glorious beaches as well as resorts. **Tramore**, Co Waterford, has a wide sweep of beach and the resort offers the amusement park and much more to entertain.

Boat trips/watersports

Most children love a boat trip. In Glengarriff, Co Cork, boatmen vie for the privilege of transporting summer visitors to **Garinish Island** in Bantry Bay (*see p74*). Seals are often seen basking on rocks. Italian gardens are the big attraction on the island. Children can explore woodland paths, a Grecian temple and a Martello tower.

There's another interesting boat cruise on **Killarney's Lower Lake**.

Sea canoeing is also an option. In Kenmare in Co Kerry, **Star Outdoors** (*tel: (064) 664 1222; www.star outdoors.ie*) offers a sheltered, supervised bay where children can practise their canoeing skills in safety.

Caves

Caves are always fascinating. Among the most dramatic are **Marble Arch**

If your children are brave, try Carrick-a-Rede Rope Bridge

Caves (*see p114*) – and **Aillwee Cave**, Ballyvaughan, Co Clare, long ago inhabited by brown bears (*see p79*).

Horse riding

Ireland has residential riding centres where instruction is given, or where trail riding is offered. There are also non-residential centres which take novices, including children, for basic instruction by the hour.

Museums

Belfast's **Ulster Folk and Transport Museum** may appeal to children, and on Saturdays in summer a miniature railway operates (*see p109*).

Zoos and wildlife

Belfast Zoo is situated on Cave Hill (*see p98*). **Dublin Zoo**, in Phoenix Park, opened more than 170 years ago (*see p32*).

The **Ark Open Farm** in Newtownards gives visitors the chance to see over 80 rare breeds of domesticated animal as well as common farm animals (*see p106*).

Westport House, Westport, Co Mayo, has a small animal collection and a wonderfully equipped children's playground (*see p87*).

Visitors can observe the milking routine, see animals and also follow a nature trail at **Streamvale**. This is Northern Ireland's first open dairy farm (*Ballyhanwood Rd, Dundonald, Belfast; tel: (028) 9048 3244; www.streamvale.com*).

Sport and leisure

Ireland generally manages to maintain a reasonably high profile in international sports – especially rugby and football – but traditional games continue to attract a huge following. The most striking characteristics of traditional games are the fervour and sportsmanship of the players and the exemplary behaviour of the fans.

Spectator sports

While Ireland is just as football-mad as the rest of Europe, it has its own distinctive and very popular games: hurling, Gaelic football, camogie and even road bowling are followed by dedicated and loyal supporters, many of whom enjoy a flutter on the outcome of their favourite games. Catching a good Gaelic football or hurling match while visiting Ireland is well worth the effort.

Gaelic football

Gaelic football, a hybrid of soccer and rugby, is played with a round ball and involves two 15-strong teams whose members may handle the ball. The third Sunday in September is the All-Ireland final. During the weekends of August and September, Dublin fills with the colour of the county teams. Green and gold of Kerry, red and white of Tyrone and orange and white of Armagh are the colours you are most likely to see as the final approaches.

Horse racing

Ireland has 26 courses, offering racing over 250 days of the year. Sunday racing has been introduced in recent years, and evening meetings are held from May to August. The headquarters of Irish racing is the Curragh, Co Kildare, where the Dubai Duty Free Irish Derby is run in June. Another classic, the Irish Oaks, is held at the Curragh in July.

The Irish Grand National event takes place at Fairyhouse, Co Meath, at Easter. Other National Hunt courses are at Galway, Gowran Park, Navan and Punchestown. The Irish Point-to-Point season of rural steeplechases runs from January to May.

A calendar giving full details of racing is available from **Horse Racing Ireland** (*Ballymany, The Curragh, Co Kildare; tel: (045) 455455; www.go racing.ie*).

In Northern Ireland the major event is the Ulster National steeplechase, staged in February/ March at Downpatrick.

The Irish National Stud and the Irish Horse Museum are both at Tully, Co Kildare (*tel: (045) 521617; www. irish-national-stud.ie*). The museum tells the story of the Irish horse from prehistoric times. Its centrepiece is the skeleton of the famous racehorse Arkle.

Hurling

The national game is hurling. An ancient game – it is mentioned in early Irish legends – hurling looks like a cross between rugby, hockey, lacrosse and guerrilla warfare. Played between teams of 15 burly men (there is a women's version, called camogie), it is said to be the world's fastest field game. The players belt a small leather ball with hockey-like sticks. The ball may be caught but not thrown. Hurling fields, found all over the Republic and in some parts of Northern Ireland, look like rugby pitches except that goalposts are netted below the crossbar. The All-Ireland final is the third Sunday in September. Cork (red and white), Galway (maroon and white) and Kilkenny (gold and black stripes) are the top teams.

Road bowls

Popular in Cork and Armagh, competitors hurl a heavy steel ball to an agreed point in the smallest number of throws.

Rugby

Local matches are played at weekends throughout the Republic and Northern Ireland. In Dublin, international matches take place at the Lansdowne Road stadium (currently undergoing rebuilding). The atmosphere in Dublin during rugby weekends is electric. Details of fixtures can be found in the national and local press.

Showjumping

Showjumping is one of Ireland's main weekend attractions, with more than 500 events taking place each year, some held in conjunction with agricultural shows. Country shows offer an attractive spectacle and provide an insight into Irish rural life. A full list of shows is available from **Showjumping Ireland** (*Beech House, Millennium Park, Oberstown, Naas, Co Kildare; tel: (045) 852230; www.sji.ie*).

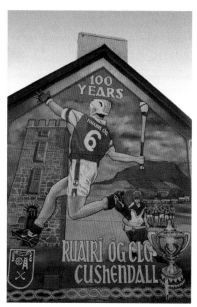

Hurling mural in Cushendall, Co Antrim

Skittles

Another traditional game now being revived in Ulster is crossroads skittles. Popular before the advent of television in Cavan, Donegal, Fermanagh, Leitrim and Monaghan, the game is re-emerging at fairs and festivals and championships have been staged in Co Fermanagh.

Participatory sports

Fresh air and fitness are easy to find in Ireland, where the opportunities for outdoor pursuits are many and varied. Indoor facilities – swimming pools and gyms – are found in many luxury and resort hotels.

Adventure pursuits

Mountains in Ireland are mostly well-rounded ranges rather than high jagged peaks, which means an absence of vicious air currents.

Add the facts that most of the hills are free of trees, power lines and other encumbrances, and that many of them provide a soft landing on peat, and it is clear that Ireland has near-ideal conditions for **gliding** and **hang-gliding**. On good days pilots can enjoy soaring for hours at a time. There are guided tours between March and September and tuition is available.

Parachuting, which for the dedicated enthusiast can lead to **skydiving**, takes place at weekends in Ireland's two centres. A first-timer can jump from an aircraft after a day's training.

Few hills and mountains of Ireland exceed 920m (3,020ft), but they provide interesting **climbing**, beauty and solitude. Mountain rescue teams with helicopter backup operate in the main areas. Because there are few tracks, maps and compasses should always be carried. Also keep in mind that the weather changes abruptly, without warning.

Canoeing is one of Ireland's fastest-growing sports, on coastal and inland waters. It takes place all year. As well as touring and camping by canoe – the option of most visitors – there are summer marathons, flat-water sprints, and, for the highly skilled, surfing.

White-water racing – timed runs over very rough stretches of river – and slaloms are other exciting aspects of canoeing, and can be enjoyable spectator sports too.

USEFUL ADDRESSES

Irish Hang Gliding and Paragliding Association (*www.ihpa.ie*) has information on sites, safety, hire and sale, and regulations for visitors to Ireland, but users must be registered to use some parts of the website.
Mountaineering Ireland (*tel: (01) 625 1115; www.mountaineering.ie*) has safety information and an excellent list of loop walks throughout the Republic, links to rock-climbing clubs and much more.
Irish Canoe Union (*www.canoe.ie*) has lists of canoeing clubs throughout Ireland as well as information on white-water racing.
The Parachute Association of Ireland (*67 Craddockstown Way, Naas, Co. Kildare; www.thepai.ie*) has lists of parachuting clubs and local safety information.

Equestrian sports

Ireland and the horse are closely linked and there are riding centres, residential and non-residential, everywhere you go. Even those visitors staying in Dublin or Belfast will not have far to travel to get into the saddle.

Among the establishments in the Dublin area are the **Carrickmines Equestrian Centre** (*Glenamuck Rd, Foxrock; tel: (01) 295 5990; www.carrick minesequestrian.ie*), and **Brooke Lodge Riding Centre** (*Burrow Rd, Stepaside; tel: (01) 295 2153*).

In the south, **Long's Trekking Centre** organises various horse-riding activities from an hour's hire to a day's trek in the Dingle Peninsula (*Ventry, Co Kerry; tel: (066) 915 9723; www.longsriding.com*).

Trail riding, where overnight accommodation is provided in farmhouses, country homes and hotels, or at stay-put centres, is available in many rural areas. Arrangements can also be made for visitors to participate in hunting.

More detailed information on riding holidays can be obtained from any Irish Tourist Board or Northern Ireland Tourist Board office, or from the **Association of Irish Riding Establishments** (*11 Moore Park, Newbridge, Co Kildare; tel: (045) 850800; www.aire.ie*).

Fishing

Few countries offer such a profusion of well-stocked fishing waters as Ireland, and few market their angling facilities so expertly or so affordably. Festivals and competitions in coarse, game and sea angling are open for visitors. Sea angling and coarse fishing are year-round activities in Ireland.

Walking is an adventure atop the Cliffs of Moher

For fishing in private water, the permission of the owner must be obtained. A licence may be required for game fishing, but licences are not needed for sea fishing.

In the Republic be sure to stay at accommodation registered with and approved by Bord Fáilte (Irish Tourist Board). Specialist accommodation offers such amenities as meals served to suit ideal local fishing times, copious hot water, a rod room and overnight clothes drying. Your game-fish catch can be deep-frozen or smoked to take home.

The Central Fisheries Board (An Príomh Bhord Iascaigh) has an excellent website, *www.cfb.ie*, which offers detailed information on good fishing sites for coarse, sea, pike, trout, salmon and sea trout, as well as lists of ghillies, boats and equipment for hire. It also has details on permits and fishing for anglers with a disability. Another excellent website is *www. discoverireland.ie/what-to-do/ Activities-and-Adventure/Angling/ Anglers-Welcome*, which, besides locations for angling, has lists

---

USEFUL ADDRESSES

National Coarse Fishing Federation of Ireland
'Blaithín', Dublin Rd, Cavan.
Tel: (049) 433 2367.
Irish Federation of Sea Anglers
67 Windsor Drive, Monkstown, Co Dublin.
Tel: (01) 280 6873.
Trout Anglers Federation of Ireland
Burkes Boats, Castlebar Rd, Ballinrobe,
Co Mayo. Tel: (094) 954 1324.

---

of specialist accommodation geared towards angling holidays, angling schools and tackle shops.

In Northern Ireland, *www.dcal-fishingni.gov.uk* suggests some good fishing locations and has information about fishing permits, and *www. discovernorthernireland.com/angling* has information on locations and regulations. The Northern Ireland Tourist Board issues free guides, available from the Belfast Welcome Centre or any of the tourist offices in Northern Ireland, to the various types of accommodation in the north, though none specifically dedicated to anglers.

Golf

There are over 350 golf courses in Ireland that welcome visitors. Those in the Dublin area include the **Royal Dublin Golf Club** (*North Bull Island, Dollymount; tel: (01) 833 6346; book online at www.theroyaldublingolf club.com*), and the Arnold Palmer-designed **K Club** (*Straffan, Co Kildare; tel: (01) 601 7200; www.kclub.com*). Belfast has about a dozen clubs within 8km (5 miles) of the city centre. Information is available from the **Golfing Union of Ireland** (*Carton Demesne, Maynooth, Co Kildare; tel: (01) 505 4000; www.gui.ie*).

Sailing and watersports

Ireland's varied coastline – to say nothing of its many lakes – offers everything from windsurfing and

Lobster fishing at Sandycove

dinghy-sailing to sedate cruising and rugged ocean racing.

The most popular cruising area, between Cork Harbour and the Dingle Peninsula, offers 143 totally different places where a boat can moor safely and peacefully for an overnight stay. Harbours like Youghal, Dunmore East and Kinsale extend a welcome to yachtsmen in their friendly bars and restaurants.

Sailing schools are located at a number of places on the Irish Sea and Atlantic coasts. For further information contact the **Irish Sailing Association** (*3 Park Rd, Dun Laoghaire, Co Dublin; tel: (01) 280 0239; www.sailing.ie*).

The Irish Tourist Board issues a leaflet with details of yacht charter companies. In Northern Ireland, the **Fermanagh Tourist Information Centre** (*Wellington Rd, Enniskillen, Co Fermanagh; tel: (028) 6632 3110*)

has information on watersports facilities on Lough Erne.

Surfing and windsurfing have become very popular in Ireland in recent years. Some Irish beaches offer world-class facilities. For further information on surfing go to *www.isasurf.ie*. See *www.windsurfing.ie* for more information on windsurfing.

Tennis

Although the Irish climate is often unsympathetic, tennis is growing in popularity. Public courts can be found in the cities and larger towns, and about 100 hotels have grass or hard courts.

Dublin is well served, with public facilities at **Bushy Park** (*tel: (01) 490 0320*), **Herbert Park** (*tel: (01) 668 4364*) and **St Anne's Park** (*tel: (01) 833 8898*). For further information, contact **Tennis Ireland** (*Dublin City University, Glasnevin, Dublin 9; tel: (01) 884 4010; www.tennisireland.ie*).

Food and drink

Places to eat out in the Republic and Northern Ireland vary from coffee shops and pubs to high-class restaurants and the occasional castle offering medieval-style dining. Generally, prices are lower in the North. It is wise to book in advance or arrive early for anything but the most casual of evening meals – this applies particularly on Sundays in the North where some places are closed.

Some restaurants, including those in hotels in both the North and the Republic, serve food nearly all day – lunches, snacks and high tea – then close their dining room at 7pm or 8pm. Except in the fashionable parts of major cities, people tend to eat early.

Expect to pay around €4.30 plus for a pint of Guinness® – other stouts may be cheaper.

In the restaurants recommended in the following list, the **£** rating indicates the approximate cost for a three-course evening meal per person, excluding wine or coffee except where stated. Service charges vary, so check the menu.

£	under €30
££	€30–€40
£££	€40–€50
££££	over €50

Good Food Ireland (*www.goodfoodireland.ie*) is one of the best specialist guides available.

LEINSTER
Dublin City
Avoca Café £
Delicious home-made dishes at the café upstairs in the retail outlet.
11–13 Suffolk St, Dublin 2. Tel: (01) 672 6019. www.avoca.ie. Open: Mon–Wed, Fri & Sat 10am–5pm, Thur 10am–6pm, Sun 11am–5pm.

Café Fresh £
Delicious vegetarian food that will send you to the bookshop for *The Café Fresh Cookbook* by Mary Farrell.
Powerscourt Townhouse Centre, South William St, Dublin 2. Tel: (01) 671 9669. www.cafe-fresh.com. Open: Mon–Fri 10am– 6pm, Sat 9am–6pm.

Cornucopia £
Gives a whole new meaning to vegetarian cuisine. Excellent, inexpensive, tasty food.
19 Wicklow St, Dublin 2. Tel: (01) 677 7583. www.cornucopia.ie. Open: Mon–Wed noon–9pm, Thur–Sat noon–10.30pm, Sun noon–8.30pm.

Mao's £
Excellent Asian restaurant.
2–3 Chatham Row,

Dublin 2.
Tel: (01) 670 2131.
www.cafemao.com

O'Neill's £
Three centuries of
serving customers good
food and drink. Pub
grub and much more.
2 Suffolk St, Dublin 2.
Tel: (01) 679 3656.
www.oneillsbar.com

Silk Road Café £
Excellent fare beside
Chester Beatty Library in
an enclosed courtyard.
Great for lunches or just
a coffee. Self-service.
Dublin Castle, Dublin 2.
Tel: (01) 407 0770.
www.silkroadcafe.ie.
Open: summer daily until
4.30pm (food served until
4pm).

Soup Dragon £
Great selection of soups
for lunch.
168 Capel St.
Tel: (01) 872 3277.
www.soupdragon.com.
Open: Mon–Fri until
5pm, Sat until 4pm.

Botticelli's ££
Simple, relaxed,
family-run Italian
restaurant with great
atmosphere.
3 Temple Bar, Dublin 2.
Tel: (01) 672 7289.
www.botticelli.ie

Boulevard Cáfe ££
Relaxed Italian/
European-style bistro.
27 Exchequer St,
Dublin 2.
Tel: (01) 679 2131.
www.boulevardcafe.ie

Browne's ££
Simple interior but
excellent French-style
cuisine in this small
place, by day a café and
by night filled with happy
locals. Works by local
artists are on display.
Bring your own wine.
18 Sandymount Green,
Sandymount, Dublin 4.
Tel: (01) 269 7316.

The Cedar Tree ££
Lebanese cuisine and
vegetarian dishes in
Arabian-style 'cavern'.
11a St Andrew's St,
Dublin 2.
Tel: (01) 677 2121.

Chandni's Restaurant ££
Good tandoori food
accompanied by sitar
music.
174 Pembroke Rd,
Ballsbridge, Dublin 4.
Tel: (01) 668 9088.
Open: Mon–Fri lunch,
daily until late.

**Montys of
Kathmandu ££**
Famous Nepalese
restaurant.

28 Eustace St, Temple Bar,
Dublin 2.
Tel: (01) 670 4911.
www.montys.ie

**O'Connell's in
Donnybrook ££**
Something for everybody
at affordable prices.
Locally sourced, well-
cooked, inventive food
served all day.
135 Morehampton Rd,
Dublin. Tel: (01) 269
6116. www.oconnells
donnybrook.com

Eden £££
Lovely, locally sourced,
imaginative food in a
bright, modern setting.
Cook for yourself with
the Eden Cookbook by
Eleanor Walsh and
Michael Durkin.
Sycamore St, Temple Bar,
Dublin 2.
Tel: (01) 670 5372.
www.edenrestaurant.ie

Chapter One ££££
Long-established, classy
place serving modern
Irish cuisine using
locally sourced
ingredients. Catch the
very popular pre-theatre
dinner menu from 6pm
to 7.45pm and get great
food at reduced prices.
18–19 Parnell Square
North, Dublin 1.

Tel: (01) 873 2266.
www.chapterone
restaurant.com. Open:
Tue–Fri lunch, Tue–Sat
dinner.

Roly's Bistro ££££

Traditional and modern
Irish mix. Delicious food,
good service and great
atmosphere.
7 Ballsbridge Terrace,
Dublin 4.
Tel: (01) 668 2611.
www.rolysbistro.ie

The Saddle Room ££££

Lovely place for a
romantic dinner for two
or an evening out with
friends and family. This
place has the confidence
and space to cater for
anyone's needs. Two
courses for lunch is easily
affordable and adequate.
The Shelbourne Hotel,
27 St Stephen's Green,
Dublin 2.
Tel: (01) 663 4500.

The Tea Room ££££

Classically influenced,
innovative cuisine in a
grand, elegant dining
room. A special-occasion
place. Choose the
market menu for a less
expensive meal.
6–8 Wellington Quay,
Dublin 2. Tel: (01) 407
0800. www.theclarence.ie

Co Carlow

The Lord Bagenal Restaurant ££

Set in a classy four-star
boutique hotel, the
restaurant is all cosy log
fires and traditional Irish
food. Check out the
Waterfront Restaurant in
the same building for its
views and innovative
cooking.
Main St, Leighlinbridge.
Tel: (059) 972 1668.
www.lordbagenal.com

Co Dublin

Alexis £

Excellent food and very
popular. Small menu but
great-value early-bird
choices. Vegetarians
might struggle a little.
Not a place for a
romantic night out as
it can get noisy.
17–18 Patrick St,
Dun Laoghaire. Tel: (01)
280 8872. www.alexis.ie

Nosh £–££

Very popular restaurant
where you'll have to fight
the regulars for a table.
Simple, modern Irish
with European twinges.
Children's menu. The
smaller early-bird menu,
available all evening
(Fri & Sat until 7.45pm),
is less exciting but great
value.
111 Coliemore Rd,
Dalkey. Tel: (01) 284
0666. www.nosh.ie.
Closed: Mon.

Cape Greko ££

Hidden away upstairs
above a pizza place, this
is a little bit of Cyprus at
the Irish seaside. All the
Greek classics, lots of
vegetarian options,
children welcome before
9pm, and music on
Friday nights. The early-
bird menu makes it a
good bargain to boot.
Who needs a view when
you've got all this?
Unit 1, First Floor, New
St, Malahide. Tel: (01)
845 6288.
www.capegreko.ie

Aqua Restaurant £££

Set in the old yacht club,
this restaurant has the
most amazing views and
good service. Well-
cooked, largely seafood
dishes, but with choices
for both carnivores and
vegetarians. The early-
bird menu or mid-week
specials are good
bargains.
1 West Pier, Howth.
Tel: (01) 832 0690.
www.aqua.ie. Closed: Mon.

Cavistons £££

Fantastic fresh fish dishes. Usually lunch only, but well worth booking a seat for Friday or Saturday evening.
59 Glasthule Rd, Sandycove.
Tel: (01) 280 9245.
www.cavistons.com

Ella's £££

If a place is popular with locals, you know it makes sense. Well-cooked, reasonably priced food in this intimate wine bar.
7 Main St, Howth.
Tel: (01) 839 6264.
www.ellawinebar.com

Bon Appetit ££££

Two restaurants in one – downstairs is casual, bistro-style food at good value, and upstairs is *haute* in many senses of the word. A Michelin-starred chef offers a fine-dining experience. You need some sturdy plastic to try the Menu Prestige.
9 St James Terrace, Malahide.
Tel: (01) 845 0314.
www.bonappetit.ie.
Closed: Sun.

King Sitric ££££

Well-established, excellent fish restaurant with glorious views.
East Pier, Harbour Rd, Howth.
Tel: (01) 832 5235.
www.kingsitric.ie

Redbank Guesthouse and Restaurant ££££

Chef/proprietor cooks catch of the day, landed at the pier each evening. Try the value-for-money early-bird at 6pm.
6–7 Church St, Skerries.
Tel: (01) 849 1005.
www.redbank.ie.
Open: Mon–Sat dinner, Sun lunch.

Co Kildare

Flanagan's ££

This popular bar in the Silken Thomas pub does a huge range of food, from filled panini to steaks, pasta and more substantial dishes. You could check out the new Chapter 13 Restaurant in the same establishment for a more formal meal.
The Silken Thomas, The Square, Kildare.
Tel: (045) 522232.
www.silkenthomas.com

Castle ££££

Formal dining in the Castle's dining room.
Barberstown Castle, Straffan.
Tel: (01) 628 8157.
www.barberstowncastle.ie.
Open: for dinner Fri–Sat.

Co Kilkenny

Marble City Bar ££

Bistro-style food in this stylish, dark bar and restaurant serving modern Irish cuisine.
66 High St, Kilkenny.
Tel: (056) 776 1143.
www.langtons.ie

Campagne £££

Worth making the trip to Kilkenny for, this place is sharp, modern and does delicious food. If you feast between 6pm and 7pm, you can eat lovely, lovely food at one-star prices.
The Arches, 5 Gashouse Lane, Kilkenny.
Tel: (056) 777 2858.
www.campagne.ie.
Open: Tue–Sat dinner, Fri–Sun lunch.

Co Westmeath

Gallery 29 Café ££

Café and bakery with good lunch menu served till 6pm.
16 Oliver Plunkett St, Mullingar.
Tel: (044) 934 9449.
Closed: Sun–Wed.

**The Wineport
Restaurant ££££**
Great lakeside location.
Booking advised.
*Glasson Village.
Tel: (090) 643 9010.
www.wineport.ie*

Co Wexford
La Dolce Vita ££
Italian restaurant with
big reputation. Worth
seeking out for lunch or
dinner on Saturday.
*6–7 Trimmers Lane,
Wexford. Tel: (053) 917
0806. Closed: Sun.*

**Beaches Restaurant,
Kelly's Hotel £££**
Excellent restaurant
in a family-run hotel.
Reservations
recommended.
*Rosslare.
Tel: (053) 913 2114.
www.kellys.ie*

Co Wicklow
**Avoca Café at The Old
Mill £**
One of several Avoca
cafés offering renowned
self-service food, this
one in the fictional
Ballykissangel; in reality
Avoca village.
*The Old Mill, Avoca.
Tel: (0402) 35105.
www.avoca.ie*

The Hungry Monk ££
Unusual, with good
wholesome cooking and
an excellent wine list.
The cheaper menu in the
bistro is great value.
*Greystones.
Tel: (01) 287 5759.
www.thehungrymonk.ie*

MUNSTER
Co Clare
Crotty's £
Pub/guesthouse noted for
simple fare and legendary
traditional music
sessions. Serves lunch and
dinner daily.
*The Square, Kilrush.
Tel: (065) 905 2470.
www.crottyspubkilrush.
com*

**The Gallery
Restaurant ££**
Thoughtful and varied
menu in quaint, stone-
built house. Good wine
list and an early-bird
menu.
*Main St, Quin.
Tel: (065) 682 5789.
Open: Tue–Sun
5.30–10pm Sun lunch.*

Co Cork
Farmgate Café £
Seasonal vegetables from
the covered market
downstairs and

traditional food of Cork.
*Old English Market,
Princes St, Cork.
Tel: (021) 427 8134.
Open: Mon–Sat breakfast
& lunch.*

An Sugán ££
Popular town-centre pub
and restaurant. Bread
baked on the premises,
fresh fish caught locally
and, of course, the local
black pudding.
*41 Wolfe Tone St,
Clonakilty.
Tel: (023) 883 3719.
www.ansugan.com*

Ballymaloe House £££
Traditional food using
prime local ingredients.
*Shanagarry, East Cork.
Tel: (021) 465 2531.
www.ballymaloe.ie*

Barn Restaurant £££
Fresh Irish produce,
distinctive cuisine.
*Lotamore, Glanmire.
Tel: (021) 486 6211.
www.barn-
restaurant.com*

Café Paradiso £££
Top vegetarian food.
*16 Lancaster Quay,
Western Rd, Cork.
Tel: (021) 427 7939.
www.cafeparadiso.ie*

Finins £££
Quality food, bar menu.
75 Main St, Midleton.

Tel: (021) 463 1878.
Closed: Sun.

Fishy Fishy Café £££
Very popular, award-winning restaurant with a reputation for excellent cooking and very fresh seafood. Make a reservation if you can, or be prepared to queue.
Crowley's Quay,
Kinsale.
Tel: (021) 470 0415.
www.fishyfishy.ie

Gleesons £££
A wide-reaching menu and lots of locally produced food.
Strand House, Clonakilty.
Tel: (023) 21834.

Heron's Cove £££
Delicious dishes in a great setting.
Goleen, near Schull,
West Cork.
Tel: (028) 35225.
www.heronscove.com

Jacob's Ladder £££
Irish cooking and great views over Cobh Harbour.
WatersEdge Hotel,
Cobh, East Cork.
Tel: (021) 481 5566.

The Spinnaker £££
Modern Irish cuisine, great views and friendly, welcoming staff. Lots of very fresh seafood,
as well as steaks and vegetarian options. Early-bird is good value.
Scilly, Kinsale.
Tel: (021) 477 2098.
www.harbourlodge.com

Co Kerry

Jam £
Café/bakery/deli set in a quiet pedestrianised laneway. Outdoor seating. Great place for lunch or high tea.
Old Market Lane,
Killarney.
Tel: (064) 37716.
www.jam.ie

Killarney Royal Hotel ££
Good for lunch or dinner.
College St, Killarney.
Tel: (064) 31853.
www.killarneyroyal.ie

The Moorings ££
Lovely, out-of-the-way bar and restaurant, ideally situated for a visit to the Skellig Islands. Mostly seafood, but carnivores and vegetarians have options too.
Portmagee.
Tel: (066) 947 7108.
www.moorings.ie

The Global Village £££
Long-established place with a great
reputation serving a very eclectic range of dishes. If you enjoy eating fast and early the early-bird menu is great value for money.
Upper Main St, Dingle.
Tel: (066) 915 2325. www.
globalvillagedingle.com.
Closed: mid-Nov–Mar.

The Lime Tree £££
Very popular modern Irish restaurant. Book a table in advance.
Shelburne St,
Kenmare.
Tel: (064) 41225. www.
limetreerestaurant.com.
Closed: Oct–Mar.

Co Limerick

Aubars ££
Good value, sound reputation. Casual dining upstairs or just come for a drink and snack in the bar.
49 Thomas St, Limerick.
Tel: (061) 317799.
www.aubars.com

Patrick Punch's ££
Roasts, prime steaks, seafood.
Punch's Cross,
Limerick.
Tel: (061) 460800.
www.patrickpunchs
hotel.com

The Wild Geese £££
Modern Irish cooking.
Adare. Tel: (061) 396451.
www.thewild-geese.com.
Open: Tue–Sat; winter
Tue–Sat dinner.

Co Tipperary
Befani's ££
Come here to graze on
the tapas or enjoy a
Mediterranean-style
meal. The early-bird
menu is excellent value.
6 Sarsfield St, Clonmel.
Tel: (052) 617 7893.
www.befani.com
Cherry Tree
Restaurant £££
Simple organic dishes
exquisitely cooked.
Killaloe.
Tel: (061) 375688. www.
cherrytreerestaurant.ie

Co Waterford
Harlequin Café &
Winebar £
Little gem of a place with
inexpensive, small menu
and some excellent wines.
37 Stephen St, Waterford.
Tel: (051) 877552.
www.harlequin-cafe.com
Azzurro ££
Italian menu includes
vegetarian and seafood.
Check out the early-
bird menu.

Dunmore East, Waterford.
Tel: (051) 383141.
Restaurant Chez K's ££
Locally sourced,
innovative food.
Vegetarians welcome.
Bridge St, Waterford.
Tel: (051) 846900.
www.fitzwiltonhotel.ie
Waterford Castle ££££
Chef Michael Quinn uses
local organic produce in
the Munster Room
restaurant.
The Island, Ballinakill.
Tel: (051) 878203.
www.waterfordcastle.com

CONNACHT
Co Galway
Boluisce Cottage Bar ££
Award-winning seafood
bar and restaurant.
Vegetarian dishes.
Main St, Spiddal Village,
Connemara.
Tel: (091) 553286.
McDonagh's Seafood
House ££
A fish lover's dream.
Take away or eat in.
22 Quay St, Galway.
Tel: (091) 565001.
www.mcdonaghs.net.
Closed: Sun.
Pangur Bán ££
Great restaurant food in
an old thatched cottage.
Fish dishes and speciality

duck are recommended.
Letterfrack.
Tel: (095) 41243.
www.pangurban.com
Peacockes ££
Fresh fish and quality
steaks reasonably priced.
Maam Cross.
Tel: (091) 552306.
www.peacockes.ie
Pier House ££
Contemporary Irish
cuisine made with local
ingredients. Seafood
oriented, but with other
options. Make a
reservation for dinner.
Kilronan, Inishmore,
Aran Islands.
Tel: (099) 61417.
www.pierhousearan.com.
Closed: Oct–Mar.
Fisherman's
Cottage ££–£££
Small menu, carefully
cooked in idyllic
rural setting. Worth
seeking out.
Inishere, Aran Islands.
Tel: (099) 75073.
www.southaran.com.
Closed: Jun–Sept Mon,
Oct–May.
Owenmore
Restaurant £££
Country house serving
fresh home-made dishes;
local seafood a speciality.
Ballynahinch Castle

Hotel, Recess, Connemara.
Tel: (095) 31006. www.
ballynahinch-castle.com.
Closed: Feb.

Paddy Burkes £££

Connoisseurs should
experience the
Clarenbridge oyster
here.

The Oyster Inn,
Clarenbridge.
Tel: (091) 796226. www.
paddyburkesgalway.com

Co Sligo

Montmartre £££

Imaginative French
cuisine with a great
reputation. Check out
the early-bird menu.
1 Market Yard, Sligo.
Tel: (071) 916 9901. www.
montmartrerestaurant.ie.
Open: Tue–Sat dinner.

ULSTER
Belfast

Archana £

This place survived all
the years of tumult in the
city and has been turning
out brilliant, authentic
Indian food for years.
Vegetarians will think
they died and went to
heaven.
53 Dublin Rd, Belfast.
Tel: (028) 9032 3713.
www.archana.co.uk

Café Renoir £

Popular pizza joint
with lots more
home-baked goodies
on offer, from breakfast
until very late.
95 Botanic Ave, Belfast.
Tel: (028) 9031 1300.
www.caferenoir.net

Cargoes Café £

Operating long before
Lisburn Road became
the trendy place it is, this
café offers a lovely mixed
European and Asian
menu. Good veggie
choices.
613 Lisburn Rd, Belfast.
Tel: (028) 9066 5451.
Closed: Sun.

Green's Pizzeria £

Pretty good pizza joint
that also does some pasta
dishes. Bring your own
wine for an inexpensive
meal. You can also
design your own pizza.
549 Lisburn Rd, Belfast.
Tel: (028) 9066 6033.
www.greenspizza.com.
Open: daily for dinner,
Fri–Sun lunch.

Beatrice Kennedy's ££

Unusual range of
delicious dishes.
44 University Rd, Belfast.
Tel: (028) 9020 2290.
www.beatricekennedy.
co.uk

Bourbon ££

Steaks, pizzas and
seafood; booking
advisable, especially
at weekends.
60 Great Victoria St,
Belfast. Tel: (028) 9033
2121. www.bourbon
restaurant.com

Deane's at Queen's ££

The third jewel in the
crown of the Deane
empire. Set in the
university with outdoor
seating, a children's
menu and a casual
atmosphere.
36 College Gardens,
Belfast.
Tel: (028) 903 8211.
www.michaeldeane.co.uk

Deane's Deli ££

New York-style deli and
a retail store for the
restaurateur's branded
products.
44 Bedford St, Belfast.
Tel: (028) 9024 8800.

Errigle Inn ££

Good, standard pub
food, live music, roof
garden.
320 Ormeau Rd, Belfast.
Tel: (028) 9064 1410.
www.errigle.com

Ginger ££

Bistro-style eatery, good
for lunch.
7 Hope St, Belfast.

Tel: (028) 9024 4421.
www.gingerbistro.com.
Open: Mon–Sat dinner,
Tue–Sat lunch.

Madison's ££

Lively bar and restaurant
near the university; the
seasonal bistro menu
ranges from steaks and
seafood to vegetarian
dishes.
59–63 Botanic Ave,
Belfast.
Tel: (028) 9050 9800.
www.madisonshotel.com

Metro Brasserie ££

Hotel restaurant with a
solid reputation and a
separate vegetarian
menu. Good early-bird
offers. Very stylish
modern cuisine.
Crescent Townhouse,
13 Lower Crescent,
Belfast. Tel: (028) 9032
0646. www.crescent
townhouse.com

Shu ££

Big, airy, modern
and very popular.
Vegetarian menu too.
253 Lisburn Rd, Belfast.
Tel: (028) 9038 1655.
www.shu-restaurant.com.
Closed: Sun.

Sun Kee ££

Well-established and
popular Chinese
restaurant.

43 Donegall Pass, Belfast.
Tel: (028) 9031 2016.

Villa Italia ££

Popular restaurant
with a fairly traditional
menu.
37–41 University Rd,
Belfast.
Tel: (028) 9032 8356.
www.villaitalia
restaurant.co.uk

am pm ££–£££

Popular with everyone,
providing champagne
breakfasts, quick lunches
or slow evening meals.
Upper Arthur St, Belfast.
Tel: (028) 9024 9009.
www.ampmbelfast.com

Deane's £££

Modern Irish dishes.
38 Howard St, Belfast.
Tel: (028) 9056 0000.
www.michaeldeane.co.uk

Nick's Warehouse £££

Huge barn of a place
serving intelligent
modern Irish cuisine.
Not a place for a
romantic evening for
two. Imaginative
vegetarian food.
35–39 Hill St, Belfast.
Tel: (028) 9043 9690.
www.nickswarehouse.co.uk.
Closed: Sun & Mon.

Cayenne ££££

Rankins-owned, ethnic
and Asian fusion food.

7 Ascot House,
Shaftesbury Square,
Belfast.
Tel: (028) 9033 1532.
www.cayenne-restaurant.
ie. Closed: Tue.

Co Antrim

Angelo's Ristorante £

Sound, inexpensive
Italian food.
3 Market Lane, Lisburn.
Tel: (028) 9267 2554.
Open: dinner.

Carriages £

Tasty grills and pizzas.
105 Main St, Larne.
Tel: (028) 2827 5132.
www.carriagesbistro.com.
Open: dinner.

Harbour Inn £

Fresh seafood.
5 Harbour Rd, Portrush.
Tel: (028) 7082 2430.

Jim Baker Restaurant £

Quick grills in bowling
stadium.
Ballysavage Rd, Parkgate,
Templepatrick.
Tel: (028) 9443 2937.
Closed: Jun–Jul & Sun.

Adair Arms Hotel ££

Lobster soup, snails in
garlic butter and other
delicacies à la carte.
Ballymoney Rd,
Ballymena.
Tel: (028) 2565 3674.
www.adairarms.com

Girona Restaurant ££
Close to Giant's
Causeway. Noted for
seasonal seafood specials.
Evenings only.
*The Smugglers Inn, 306
Whitepark Rd, Bushmills.
Tel: (028) 2073 1577.
www.smugglersinn
ireland.com*

The Joymount Arms ££
Bright-red pub serving
traditional, locally
sourced food.
*16–18 Joymount St,
Carrickfergus.
Tel: (028) 9336 2213.*

Londonderry Arms ££
Fresh, simple fare, home-
style cooking in former
coaching inn. Excellent
home-made bread.
*20–28 Harbour Rd,
Carnlough.
Tel: (028) 2888 5255.
www.glensofantrim.com*

Sixteenoeight ££
Popular, stylish, modern
Irish cuisine. Reservations
recommended.
*66 Main St, Bushmills.
Tel: (028) 2073 2040.
Closed: Mon & Tue.*

Bushmills Inn £££
Gas lighting, peat fires,
local products used. The
speciality here is River
Bush salmon and
Bushmills whiskey.

*9 Dunluce Rd, Bushmills.
Tel: (028) 2073 2339.
www.bushmillsinn.com*

Oregano Restaurant £££
Fresh food, locally
sourced, organic where
possible. Imaginative
dishes are well worth
seeking out in this off-
the-beaten-track place.
*29 Ballyrobert Rd,
Ballyclare. Tel: (028) 9084
0099. www.oregano
restaurant.com. Closed:
Mon.*

Co Armagh
Mandarin House £
Chinese and European.
*30 Scotch St, Armagh.
Tel: (028) 3752 2228.*

Yellow Door Deli £
Home-baked breads, fine
modern cooking. Great
place for lunch or very
early dinner.
*7 Woodhouse St,
Portadown.
Tel: (028) 3835 3528.
www.yellowdoordeli.co.uk*

**Manor Park
Restaurant ££–£££**
Renowned French
restaurant. The early-
bird menu is good value;
alcohol can trouble your
plastic, though.
*2 College Hill, Armagh.
Tel: (028) 3751 5353.*

*www.manorpark
restaurant.co.uk*

Co Donegal
The Olde Glen Bar ££
Lovely old country pub
and restaurant serving so
much more than just pub
grub. Reservation
recommended.
*Glen Carrigart.
Tel: (074) 915 5130.
Closed: summer Mon;
Oct–Mar.*

Danny Minnies £££
Locally raised or caught
produce in this classy
modern Irish restaurant.
*Teach Killindarragh,
Annagry, The Rosses.
Tel: (074) 954 8201.*

**McGrory's of
Culdaff £££**
Good food, good music
and the occasional
gourmet evening.
Modern Irish cuisine.
*Culdaff, Inishowen.
Tel: (074) 937 9104.
www.mcgrorys.ie. Closed:
Mon; winter Mon & Tue.*

Strand Hotel £££
Variety of home-cooked
dishes served in this
family-owned hotel.
*Ballyliffin.
Tel: (074) 937 6107.
www.ballyliffinstrand
hotel.com*

Water of life

Old soldiers know that you should never volunteer for anything. Old soldiers can be wrong. Lucky (or opportunist) volunteers visiting the Old Jameson Distillery in Dublin (*see p37*), or the Old Midleton Distillery at Midleton, Co Cork (*see p75*), face a rare tasting challenge – to choose their favourite from among five popular Irish whiskeys and compare them with a Scotch or Bourbon. Many people have been known to change the drinking habits of a lifetime.

Attractive signage announces the age-old drink

A gleaming copper pot still at Midleton Distillery, one of two in the country

Irish whiskey is distinctively different from Scotch whisky. In Scotland, the malted barley which forms the basis of the spirit is dried over an open peat fire, imparting its characteristic smoky flavour. The Irish dry theirs in smoke-free kilns, producing a clear, clean barley taste. Another difference is that Irish whiskey is distilled three times, while most similar spirits produced elsewhere are distilled only twice.

The art of distillation was discovered long ago in the Middle East – Aristotle mentioned the process in the 4th century BC – but it was first used for making perfume.

The Irish soon found a better use for it when distillation was introduced by Christian missionaries around AD 600. They found a good name for the new product, too – 'Water of Life'. English soldiers serving in Ireland in the 12th century shortened the Irish phrase *Uisce Beatha* (pronounced 'Ish'ke Ba-ha') to whiskey, and the word stuck.

Ireland once had more than 2,000 distilleries. Today, there are only three – at Midleton, Cooley in Louth and Bushmills, Co Antrim. Bushmills, licensed since 1608, is Ireland's oldest legal distillery (*see p119*). Like Midleton and The Old Jameson Distillery in Dublin, it has a visitor centre.

Co Down

The Bay Tree £–££

Pleasant coffee shop and café during the day, good dinner menu on Monday and Wednesday to Saturday nights.
118 High St, Holywood.
Tel: (028) 9042 1419.
www.baytreeholywood.
co.uk

Daft Eddy's £–££

A trip across the causeway is worthwhile for steak, salmon, prawns.
Sketrick Island, Killinchy, Newtownards.
Tel: (028) 9754 1615.

Curran's ££

Modern Irish cuisine in this cosy 18th-century pub.
83 Strangford Rd, Chapeltown, Ardglass.
Tel: (028) 4484 1332.
www.curransbar.net

The Duke Restaurant ££

Nice range of dishes from the exciting to the predictable. Lots of local seafood, plus more.
Duke St, Warrenpoint.
Tel: (028) 4175 2084.
Closed: Mon & Tue.

Jeffers by the Marina ££

Lovely setting and stylish food served by helpful, committed staff.
7 Gary's Hill, Bangor.
Tel: (028) 9185 9555.
www.jeffersbythemarina.
com. Closed: Mon.

Old Schoolhouse Inn ££

Interesting fresh French cuisine, traditionally cooked.
100 Ballydrain Rd, Comber.
Tel: (028) 9754 1182. www.
theoldschoolhouseinn.com

The Plough ££

Two choices of places to eat in this long-established pub and bistro. The dining room offers more traditional service while the Barretro is younger, livelier and more casual. Lunch gets pretty crowded and there are evening meals at weekends.
3 The Square, Hillsborough.
Tel: (028) 9268 2985.
www.theplough
hillsborough.co.uk

Sea Salt Deli ££

Locally sourced, interesting food. Great for lunch and sourcing a picnic. Friday and Saturday evening tapas.
51 Central Promenade, Newcastle.
Tel: (028) 4372 5027.

Co Fermanagh

Crow's Nest £

Extensive menu. Ulster breakfast all day.
12 High St, Enniskillen.
Tel: (028) 6632 5252.

Pat's Bar £

Stopping-off point for a night in the Enniskillen clubs, but has a good reputation for its pub grub. Look out for the specials.
1 Townhall St, Enniskillen.
Tel: (028) 6632 2040.
www.patsbar.co.uk

Killyhevlin
Hotel ££–£££

Two dining options in this pretty lakeside hotel. Silks offers more formal dining, and the grill and bar more casual eating.
Dublin Rd, Enniskillen.
Tel: (028) 6632 3481.
www.killyhevlin.com

Manor House Country Hotel ££–£££

Elegant dining on the shores of Lough Erne.
Killadeas.
Tel: (028) 6862 2200.
www.manor-house-
hotel.com

Co Londonderry

Ditty's Home Bakery and Coffee Shop £
Great cakes and breads and a good lunch and breakfast menu.
3 Rainey St, Magherafelt.
Tel: (028) 7963 3944.
www.dittysbakery.com

Metro Bar £
Try the beef stew.
3–4 Bank Place, Derry.
Tel: (028) 7126 7401.
Open: lunch.

The Sandwich Company £
Big, popular, lunchtime and early evening place, part of a small chain of sandwich bars serving all manner of filled breads, salads and more. If this place is full, try the one in the Diamond.
61 Strand Rd, Derry.
Tel: (028) 7126 6771.
www.thesandwichco.com

Mange 2 ££
Very popular restaurant with lovely views over the river. Nice fusion of modern and traditional cooking.
110–115 Strand Rd, Derry.
Tel: (028) 7136 1222.
www.mange2derry.com

Water Margin ££
Chinese restaurant with fine views over the river and a fantastic reputation.
The Boat House, Hanover Place, Coleraine.
Tel: (028) 7034 2222.

Brown's ££–£££
Long-established oasis of good, thoughtful cooking. Excellent early-bird menu.
1–2 Bond's Hill, Derry.
Tel: (028) 7134 5180.
www.brownsrestaurant. com. Closed: Mon.

Co Monaghan

Andy's Restaurant ££–£££
Classic bar food Tuesday to Sunday, or more formal dining in the restaurant from Wednesday to Sunday. Standard dishes enhanced by imaginative sauces.
Market St, Monaghan.
Tel: (047) 82277. www. andysmonaghan.com. Closed: Mon.

Co Tyrone

The Loft £
Set upstairs in a discount designer clothing centre, this bright, airy coffee shop is open six days a week until early evening serving sandwiches, panini and more.
The Linen Green, Moygashel.
Tel: (028) 8772 9929.

Greenvale Hotel £–££
Homely atmosphere in a converted and extended 19th-century residence.
57 Drum Rd, Cookstown.
Tel: (028) 8676 2243.
www.greenvalehotel.co.uk

Viscounts ££
Well-established restaurant set in a 19th-century church. Lots of options for dinner and lunch.
10 Northlands Row, Dungannon.
Tel: (028) 8775 3880.
www.viscounts restaurant.co.uk. Closed: Mon.

Mellon Country Hotel £££
Approximately 1.5km (1 mile) from the Ulster-American Folk Park. Paddy Brown's Restaurant serves traditional food with French accent. Non-meat dishes included in extensive menu.
134 Beltany Rd, Omagh.
Tel: (028) 8166 1224.
www.melloncountry hotel.com

Accommodation

Accommodation standards, closely watched by tourism authorities in the Republic and Northern Ireland, are improving constantly, and there's a good range – everything from internationally rated de-luxe hotels to simple hostels.

Both Bord Fáilte and the Northern Ireland Tourist Board run registration schemes with official grading systems, and both publish lists of accommodation with details of facilities and maximum prices.

The most luxurious hotel is classified as five-star and the most simple hotel classified as one-star. For guesthouses, the classification is based on the number of facilities as well as the overall standard. The top classification is four-star, with a whole range of facilities and full restaurant,

B&Bs are reasonable and not hard to find

down to one-star establishments with fewer facilities.

The best deals for hotels in Ireland are available on the Internet. There is a range of hotel booking sites; for Dublin see *www.visitdublin.com*. Alternatively, you can contact the hotel directly.

Hotels

Bord Fáilte's registered hotels range from the top-class international hotels found in Dublin and other cities and major towns to simple provincial inns. Northern Ireland has fewer actual hotels listed, but this does not present much of a problem in a province which can be spanned in any direction in less than three hours by car.

The Republic has a good range of accommodation in country houses – often elegant old manor houses or historic castles – with excellent, even luxurious, facilities. The houses are managed in many cases by the owners themselves, who go out of their way to create a house-party atmosphere. Many

Luxury hotels amid wonderful landscapes

places have indoor pools, gyms and exercise equipment, as well as excellent sporting facilities – hunting, shooting, fishing, golf – and offer high standards of cuisine.

Hidden Ireland (*PO Box 31, Westport, Co Mayo; tel: (01) 662 7166; www.hiddenireland.com*) publishes a directory of country houses. *Ireland's Blue Book*, published by **Ireland's Blue Book** (*8 Mount St Crescent, Dublin 2; tel: (01) 676 9914; www.irelandsbluebook.com*), lists a number of similar properties. Georgina Campbell's *Ireland* (*www.ireland-guide. com*) includes quality accommodation.

Guesthouses

Guesthouses are a less expensive alternative to hotels. The only difference in many cases will be in

THE SHELBOURNE

Generally accepted as 'the most distinguished address in Ireland' and one of the world's truly grand hotels, The Shelbourne, St Stephen's Green, Dublin, has been immortalised in literature, has witnessed dramatic moments in history and provided board and lodging for celebrities for almost 170 years.

William Makepeace Thackeray, George Moore and Oliver St John Gogarty all stayed at the hotel and wrote about it. Elizabeth Bowen was so enamoured of the place that she wrote a 200-page book about it, and James Joyce, who never actually stayed there, included it in 'Two Gallants', one of his *Dubliners* stories, and in his famous novel *Ulysses*. During the Easter Rising of 1916 bullets rattled against the façade as rebels and British troops battled on St Stephen's Green. Guests were quietly moved to a room at the rear to continue afternoon tea. In 1922 the Constitution of the Irish Free State was drafted in the hotel. When civil war started, The Shelbourne was again in the thick of things.

the provision of such facilities as reception areas, bars and public rooms. They consist of at least five bedrooms, often with en-suite bathrooms, and guest facilities frequently include television and direct-dial telephones.

Bed and breakfasts

B&Bs are abundant throughout the Republic and increasing in Northern Ireland. In the Republic those approved by Bord Fáilte will display a shamrock logo.

B&Bs are officially categorised as town homes, country homes or farmhouses, but they may be no bigger than a rural bungalow with a spare bedroom. However, facilities in registered B&Bs will certainly be reasonable.

Many visitors to Ireland take pot luck with B&B accommodation, choosing a place at the end of each day's touring rather than booking ahead. But it is best not to leave it too late in the day as they can fill up in the popular towns and resort areas. Useful websites are *www.townandcountry.ie* and *www.bedandbreakfastireland.net*

Farmhouses

B&Bs apart, many farms now offer holiday accommodation. Evening meals are provided in many cases if notice is given before noon.

Peace and quiet in what may well be a very isolated location are obvious attractions, but for city dwellers at least there will be the added interest of experiencing life on the farm at first hand.

Irish Farm House Holidays, Belleek Rd, Ballyshannon, Co Donegal. Tel: (071) 982 2222. www.irishfarmholidays.com

Self-catering

Self-catering accommodation covers premises ranging from bungalows, old converted houses and semi-detached homes, to modern, purpose-designed properties built and maintained to high standards by consortia.

Members of the Irish Cottage Holiday Homes Association each manage a minimum of eight purpose-built self-catering units. All are registered by Bord Fáilte and regional tourism organisations. Standards are high (though you might be expected to provide your own towels). Many properties built recently are attractive, comfortably furnished, well equipped and have plenty of parking space. Some

Charming holiday cottages in Dunmore East

A typical town-house hotel in Dublin

Hostels

An Óige, the Irish Youth Hostel Association, has 26 registered hostels, ranging from cottages and castles to former coastguard stations, schoolhouses, shooting lodges and military barracks. The hostels are available to members of the International Youth Hostels Federation (IYHF) and advance booking is advisable during the summer, especially at weekends.

Northern Ireland has six hostels run by Hostelling International Northern Ireland (HINI). There is also a large number of independent hostels throughout the country. Many are members of Independent Holiday Hostels of Ireland and provide good dormitory and private accommodation at budget prices.

An Óige, 61 Mountjoy St, Dublin 7. Tel: (01) 830 4555. www.anoige.ie HINI, 22 Donegall Rd, Belfast BT12 5JN. Tel: (028) 9032 4733. www.hini.org.uk Independent Holiday Hostels of Ireland, 57 Lower Gardiner St, Dublin 1. Tel: (01) 836 4700. www.hostels-ireland.com

Camping

There are camping and caravan sites in each of the Republic's 26 counties and in all six counties of Northern Ireland. The sites are officially regulated and inspected in the Republic and both tourist boards publish lists of sites (*see also p176*).

new properties follow traditional styles of architecture, with thatched roofs, dormer windows and stable doors.

In Northern Ireland, a downloadable brochure is available from the Northern Ireland Tourist Board. This lists accredited self-catering places – see *www.discovernorthernireland.com/downloads/NISCHA.pdf*

An option for those with grander self-catering ambitions is to rent a castle. Staff are available at some properties for those who cannot bear the thought of peeling their own potatoes or popping their own champagne corks.

Irish Cottage Holiday Homes, Bracken Court, Bracken Rd, Sandyford, Dublin. Tel: (01) 205 2777. www.irishcottageholidays.com Elegant Ireland, Box No 10871, Dublin 8. Tel: (01) 473 2505. www.elegant.ie

Accommodation

WHERE TO STAY

In the accommodation recommended in the following pages, the ratings below indicate approximate cost of a double room with breakfast.

£	under €60
££	€60–€100
£££	€100–€150
££££	€150–€250
£££££	over €250

Leinster
Dublin City
The Castle Hotel ££ This set of Georgian terraces in a relatively peaceful area offers great value for money in an expensive city. Basic, clean rooms, helpful staff and spacious public areas. Room 201 was one of Michael Collins's safe houses during the War of Independence.
2–4 Gardiner Row, Dublin 1.
Tel: (01) 874 6949. www. thecastlehotelgroup.com
Harrington Hall ££
Pretty Georgian terraced house with its own off-street parking, close to the Luas and Grafton Street.

70 Harcourt St, Dublin 2.
Tel: (01) 475 3497.
www.harringtonhall.com
The Morgan £££ In the heart of Temple Bar is this beautifully designed ultra-modern boutique hotel.
10 Fleet St, Temple Bar, Dublin 2. Tel: (01) 643 7000. www.themorgan.com
The Four Seasons £££££
Gorgeous, purpose-built hotel, with spa, pool, fitness room and all the bars and dining rooms you could ask for. Amazing service. In a quiet area of the city, ten minutes from the centre.
Simmonscourt Rd, Dublin 4.
Tel: (01) 665 4000.
www.fourseasons.com

Co Dublin
Redbank Guesthouse ££
Set in a pretty seaside village, this guesthouse is cosy, welcoming, and has an excellent restaurant.
5–7 Church St, Skerries.
Tel: (01) 849 1005.
www.redbank.ie

Co Kilkenny
Kilkenny River Court Hotel £££ Nice views of the castle; car park, pool and spa.

John St, Kilkenny.
Tel: (056) 772 3388.
www.rivercourthotel.com

Co Wexford
Kelly's Resort Hotel and Spa ££ Family-run hotel with lots of activities, set on a gorgeous sandy beach close to the ferry. Excellent restaurant.
Rosslare.
Tel: (053) 914 2779.
www.kellys.ie

Co Wicklow
Esplanade Hotel ££–£££
Victorian building on the seafront at Bray, close to the DART and pretty coastal walks.
Strand Rd, Bray.
Tel: (01) 286 2056.
www.esplanadehotel.ie

Munster
Co Clare
Gregan's Castle Hotel ££££ Luxurious small hotel, set in lovely gardens. Open fires, four-poster beds, croquet, amazing views over The Burren, excellent dining room and tasty breakfasts. Close to both Shannon and Galway Airports.

Ballyvaughan.
Tel: (065) 707 7005.
www.gregans.ie

Co Cork
Imperial Hotel ££–£££
Amid all the shiny steel
and glass of Cork's
newer hotels, this one
holds its own. Recently
brought up to date with
its own spa and pool, it
is very central and has
free parking in this
rather congested city.
South Mall, Cork. Tel:
(021) 427 4040.
www.flynnhotels.com
Perryville House £££
Pretty town house with
homely rooms and
generous public areas.
Long Quay, Kinsale.
Tel: (021) 477 2731.
www.perryvillehouse.com
Seaview House £££
Fine bedrooms and lots
of cosy spaces in this
small, family-run hotel.
Excellent restaurant,
laid-back atmosphere,
nice bar, great service.
Ballylickey, Bantry.
Tel: (027) 50462. www.
seaviewhousehotel.com
The Waterfront £££ At
the heart of the little
village of Baltimore, this
pretty guesthouse offers

neat, newly appointed
rooms. Three
restaurants, lots of sea
views and a fine boating
atmosphere.
Baltimore.
Tel: (028) 20600.
www.waterfronthotel.ie

Co Kerry
**Killarney International
Youth Hostel £** Set in
parkland, this 18th-
century manor house has
been a youth hostel for
decades. It has private,
double, en-suite rooms,
and there are kitchens,
large public areas and a
restaurant. Some distance
from town.
Aghadoe House, Ring of
Kerry Rd, Killarney.
Tel: (064) 663 1240. www.
anoige.ie
The Moorings £–££
Right beside the Skelligs
departure point, offering
bed, breakfast, a packed
lunch for the trip, and
dinner. Nice pub with
traditional music and the
best restaurant in the
area. Comfortable rooms,
though not all have good
views.
Portmagee.
Tel: (066) 947 7108.
www.moorings.ie

Pax House ££ Fine views
over Dingle Bay in this
modern, slightly out-of-
town guesthouse. Rooms
are comfortable with a
great breakfast.
Upper John St, Dingle.
Tel: (066) 915 1518.
www.pax-house.com
**Ard na Sidhe Country
House ££££** Set on the
shores of Caragh Lake on
the famous Ring of
Kerry, this beautiful
stone manor house has
18 charming bedrooms,
antique furnishings
and magical gardens
to explore.
Killorglin.
Tel: (066) 976 9105.
www.ardnasidhe.com
The Park ££££ This top-
of-the-range place is set
in secluded grounds and
boasts a gorgeous spa,
croquet on the lawn,
bicycles and stunning,
antique-filled rooms.
Kenmare.
Tel: (064) 41200.
www.parkkenmare.com

Co Tipperary
Cashel Holiday Hostel £
Private rooms in this
modern, recently
renovated hostel are en-
suite. The hostel has a

laundry, kitchen for guests' use, and is centrally located.
6 John St, Cashel.
Tel: (062) 62330.
www.cashelhostel.com

Cashel Palace Hotel £££ Once a bishop's palace, this hotel has been beautifully restored and visitors can expect a friendly, comfortable and luxurious stay. The hotel is in the centre of town, but is set back from the road with walled gardens and the bishop's private pathway to the Rock.
Main St, Cashel.
Tel: (062) 61521.
www.cashel-palace.ie

Co Waterford
Sion Hill House £££
There are only four guest rooms in this lovely old 18th-century house, the centrepiece of lovingly restored and renovated gardens. Close to Waterford city centre.
Ferrybank, Waterford.
Tel: (051) 851558.

Waterford Castle Hotel ££££ Set on a 125-hectare (310-acre) island

with its own car ferry, this is one of Ireland's most special places to stay. Like all hotels in this price range, much of what you are buying is the service and that is ladled on, from the glorious breakfasts to the nightly turn-down service.
The Island, Ballinakill, Waterford.
Tel: (051) 878203.
www.waterfordcastle.com

Connacht
Co Galway
Ardawn House ££ Big, roomy guesthouse run by committed, friendly people. Breakfasts go that extra mile.
College Rd, Galway.
Tel: (091) 568883.
www.ardawnhouse.com

Aran Islands Hotel £££ All the hotel comforts, with stunning coastal views.
Cill Ronain, Inishmore, Aran Islands.
Tel: (099) 61104. www. aranislandshotel.com

Inis Meáin Restaurant and Suites ££££ Pleasant en-suite rooms on the quietest of the Aran Islands.

Inishmaan.
Tel: (086) 826 6026.
www.inismeain.com

Co Mayo
Knockranny House Hotel £££ Modern-built, Victorian-style, roomy. Some rooms with lovely views, lots of attractive public spaces.
Knockranny, Westport.
Tel: (098) 28600.
www.khh.ie

Ashford Castle £££££ All possible luxuries, amenities, eating and pampering opportunities are here at Ireland's most gracious 13th-century castle.
Cong. Tel: (094) 954 6003. www.ashford.ie

Co Sligo
Sligo International Tourist Hostel £ For a hostel, this place hits all the right notes – clean, relatively quiet, with private singles and doubles, en-suite rooms and kitchens. Make your own breakfast.
Harbour House, Finisklin Rd, Sligo.
Tel: (071) 917 1547.
www.harbourhousehostel. com

Markree Castle £££
Affordable, if eccentric,
accommodation in a
genuine castle. Don't
expect the lap of luxury,
but enjoy genuine,
ancient rooms built on a
grand scale.
Collooney.
Tel: (071) 916 7800.
www.markreecastle.ie

Coopershill House £££££
Georgian country house
with all the luxuries set
in huge grounds
including a deer park,
tennis and croquet.
Riverstown.
Tel: (071) 916 5108.
www.coopershill.com

Ulster
Belfast
Premier Inn £ Of the
three Premier Inns in the
city, this is the most
modern. Inexpensive and
basic, it has all the things
you need for a good stay
in a city. If this one is
fully booked, try Alfred
Street or Queens Road.
2–6 Waring St, Belfast.
Tel: (0870) 423 6492.
www.premierinn.com

Hilton Hotel £££ One of
the first hotel chains to
settle in the newly
peaceful city, this place is

modern and has lovely
views over the industrial
landscape, beautiful at
night. Excellent
restaurant.
4 Lanyon Place, Belfast.
Tel: (028) 9027 7000.
www.hilton.co.uk/belfast

Co Armagh
**De Averell Guest
House ££** Comfortable,
small guesthouse right in
the city centre. Helpful,
knowledgeable owners.
*47 Upper English Street,
Armagh.*
Tel: (028) 3751 1213.
www.deaverellhouse.co.uk

Co Donegal
Donegal Manor £££
Modern building with
all the essentials and a
bit of style. Just outside
town.
Letterkenny Rd, Donegal.
Tel: (074) 972 5222.
www.donegalmanor.com

**Great Northern
Hotel £££** Big Victorian
hotel with pool, sauna,
children's area, golf
course and wonderful
beaches.
Bundoran.
Tel: (074) 1984 1204.
*www.greatnorthernhotel.
com*

Co Down
Denvir's ££ Amazing old
pub with lots of ancient
features and comfortable
rooms. The restaurant is
popular with the locals.
*14 English St,
Downpatrick.*
Tel: (028) 4461 2012.
www.denvirshotel.com

Royal Hotel ££ Nice,
family-run old hotel;
pleasant rooms, open
fires in the bar, gardens,
car park.
26 Quay St, Bangor.
Tel: (028) 9127 1866.
*www.royalhotel
bangor.com*

Co Fermanagh
Killyhevlin Hotel £££
Lovely location with
walks beside the lake.
Spa, good restaurant.
*Dublin Rd, Killyhevlin,
Enniskillen. Tel: (028)
6632 3481.*
www.killyhevlin.com

Co Londonderry
Tower Hotel ££ Recently
built, right in the heart of
Derry's ancient city.
Good restaurant, fitness
centre. Lovely views.
17–19 Butcher St, Derry.
Tel: (028) 7137 1000.
www.towerhotelderry.com

Practical guide

Arriving

Documentation

British citizens born in the UK and travelling from Britain do not need a passport to enter the Republic or Northern Ireland, but it is advisable to carry some valid official form of photo identification. Airlines insist on it. Other EU visitors to Ireland must have a passport or suitable identity documents. Citizens from the USA, Canada, Australia and New Zealand need a passport to enter either the Republic or Northern Ireland and can stay up to six months without a visa.

By air

Dublin Airport (*tel: (01) 814 1111*) is 10km (6 miles) from the city centre. Taxis are legion, but relatively expensive. **Aircoach** connects the airport with many of Dublin's top hotels (*tel: (01) 844 7118; www.aircoach.ie*). Dublin Bus operates a service to the city centre every 10–15 minutes from 6am to 11.30pm daily. Journey time is about 30 minutes (longer in rush hour). There is an express bus (No 200) from Dublin to Belfast city centre (2¾ hours).

Cork Airport is well served by Bus Éireann for the 20-minute journey to Parnell Place.

Shannon International Airport (*tel: (061) 712000*) is about 21km (13 miles) from Limerick. There are connecting flights to Dublin and other major centres. Taxis are located outside the main terminal building, and Bus Éireann Expressway has regular services to Limerick and other cities. The Limerick bus runs between 6.45am and midnight and the trip takes 45 minutes. The nearest railway station is Limerick, 2 hours 10 minutes from Dublin.

Ireland West Airport, Knock, Co Mayo, has an information centre and

A ferry leaves Dun Laoghaire Harbour

O'Connell Bridge, Dublin

car-hire facilities. There are taxis and a local bus runs to Charlestown, 11km (7 miles) away.

From Belfast International Airport, Bus 300 to Belfast, 30km (19 miles) away, departs every 20 minutes (*tel: (028) 9066 6630*). The quickest way into Belfast from Belfast City Airport is by taxi or Bus 600.

The City of Derry Airport at Eglinton is served by British Airways and Ryanair and is a useful gateway to Donegal and the northwest. Buses 143 and 234 run regularly into the city centre.

Kerry Airport has links with Luton and Stansted in the UK and Frankfurt in Germany (*tel: (066) 976 4644; www.kerryairport.com*), while Galway Airport has links with Luton and Manchester (*tel: (091) 755518; www.galwayairport.com*). Both have good bus connections into town.

By sea

Various ferry companies operate high-speed catamarans and jet-propelled craft as well as conventional vessels on ten routes between Britain and Ireland.

Using a conventional vessel, Irish Ferries takes 3¼ hours between Holyhead and Dublin and a fast ferry takes just under 2 hours. Stena Line also operates a ferry service from Holyhead to Dublin (3¼ hours) in addition to a high-speed service from Holyhead to Dun Laoghaire (1¼ hours). Both companies also run services to Rosslare – Irish Ferries from Pembroke (4 hours), Stena Line from Fishguard (3½ hours, or 1¾ hours by high-speed service).

The quickest crossings are from Scotland. Stena Line operates between Stranraer and Belfast, taking between 1½ and 3 hours. P&O European Ferries sails between Cairnryan and Larne in 1–2 hours and Troon and Larne in 2 hours.

Norfolkline Ferries takes 8½ hours between Liverpool and Belfast and 7 hours between Liverpool and Dublin. P&O does a similar Liverpool–Dublin service.

Irish Ferries has a service between Rosslare and Cherbourg (about 20 hours) and Rosslare and Roscoff (about 18 hours). Brittany Ferries runs from Cork to Roscoff, taking around 15 hours. The *Thomas Cook European Timetable* has details of ferry times. (*See* Public transport *pp185–6.*)

Camping and caravanning

Camping and caravan parks in the Republic are inspected and graded by Bord Fáilte and listed in its annual *Caravan & Camping Ireland* guide, which covers all 26 counties. The guide is available at local tourist information offices. Some parks are open year-round, but most only from May to September.

Caravan and camping parks are categorised from one- to four-stars. Touring caravans and motorhomes are also available for hire. Further details

from the **Irish Caravan and Camping Council** (*PO Box 4443, Dublin 2; www.camping-ireland.ie*).

The Northern Ireland Tourist Board lists about 44 parks in its annual guide, *Caravan and Camping in Northern Ireland*, some on sites owned by the provincial Forest Service. Visitors can stop overnight at most forest locations without a reservation, though this would be inadvisable in high season. Local tourist offices have further lists of approved caravan and camping sites. For details, contact The Forest Service (*Dundonald House (Room 34), Belfast BT4 3SB; tel: (028) 9052 4480; www. forestserviceni.gov.uk*).

Climate

Ireland's weather is rarely extreme. The coldest months are January and

WEATHER CONVERSION CHART

25.4mm = 1 inch
°F = 1.8 × °C + 32

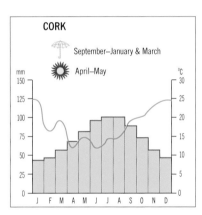

CORK

September–January & March

April–May

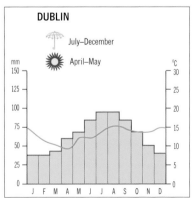

DUBLIN

July–December

April–May

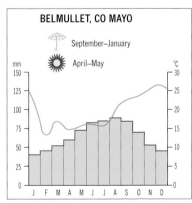

BELMULLET, CO MAYO

September–January

April–May

February, when average temperatures range from 4°C (39°F) to 7°C (45°F). In July and August the average high temperature is around 20°C (68°F).

The driest area is the coastal strip near Dublin, where the average annual rainfall is less than 750mm (30in). Rainfall in the west usually averages between 1,000mm (39in) and 1,300mm (51in), and exceeds 2,000mm (79in) in many mountainous districts. April is the driest month generally, with June the driest in many southern parts.

Conversion tables

Clothes and shoe sizes in Ireland follow the standard sizes used in the UK.

Crime

Visitors to Dublin and Belfast are advised to be careful where they park and to avoid leaving property visible in cars. Elsewhere, the island is one of the safest countries in Europe, though visitors should take the usual precautions against pickpockets or snatch-and-run thieves at large gatherings. Sensible attitudes to public places late at night and when the pubs and clubs turn out make sense throughout Ireland.

Customs regulations

Both the Republic and Northern Ireland operate schemes under which travellers from non-EU countries can claim a refund of Value Added Tax (VAT) on goods being taken abroad. Details are available at major stores.

CONVERSION TABLE

FROM	TO	MULTIPLY BY
Inches	Centimetres	2.54
Feet	Metres	0.3048
Yards	Metres	0.9144
Miles	Kilometres	1.6090
Acres	Hectares	0.4047
Gallons	Litres	4.5460
Ounces	Grams	28.35
Pounds	Grams	453.6
Pounds	Kilograms	0.4536
Tons	Tonnes	1.0160

To convert back, for example from centimetres to inches, divide by the number in the third column.

Practical guide

Driving

Drive on the left on both sides of the border. Drivers and front-seat passengers must wear seat belts, and rear seat belts must be worn where fitted.

The Republic of Ireland has three road classifications: National Primary (shown with the prefix N and numbered 1 to 25), National Secondary (prefix N, numbered over 50) and Regional (prefix R).

Northern Ireland also has three road classifications: Motorways (prefix M) and A roads and B roads.

The **AA** has a main office at *56 Drury St, Dublin 2 (tel: (01) 617 9999; www. aaireland.ie)*. The **RAC** number is *1800 535005*. Speed limits in the Republic of Ireland are now in kph. You need to be especially wary of this when you cross the border into the Republic from Northern Ireland, where speed limits are in mph.

Breakdown

Drivers of hired cars should act according to the instructions included in their documentation. If you are driving your own vehicle and are a member of the AA or one of the AIT-affiliated driving clubs, you can call on the AA rescue service on both sides of the border.

Car hire

Major international car-hire consortia are represented throughout Ireland as well as a number of smaller local firms, who also operate under a code of conduct drawn up in the Republic by Bord Fáilte and the Car Rental Council. Car hire is cheaper in Northern Ireland than in the Republic.

Dublin's Ha'penny Bridge gets its name from the toll once levied on it

Documentation

You will need a valid driving licence and, if you are bringing your own vehicle, the registration document (or a letter of authority from the vehicle owner if it is not registered in your name), plus an insurance certificate valid for either the Republic or Northern Ireland (or both).

Fuel

Fuel is marginally cheaper in the Republic of Ireland than Northern Ireland. All over Ireland there are 24-hour petrol stations.

Insurance

Fully comprehensive cover is best, with collision damage waiver (CDW) if renting. Travel insurance does not usually cover travellers for third-party liability arising out of the use of a car; if you are hiring one, check that this is included in the hirer's insurance, or purchase a top-up policy before you travel. Check that insurance covers the Republic and Northern Ireland if you intend to cross the border.

Maximum speed limits

Republic of Ireland:
- National Primary roads 120kph/74mph
- National Secondary roads 100kph/62mph; regional and local roads 80kph/50mph
- 50kph/31mph built-up areas
- 80kph/50mph vehicles towing trailers

Northern Ireland:
- 112kph/70mph dual carriageways and motorways
- 96kph/60mph country areas
- 48kph/30mph built-up areas

In Northern Ireland speed limits are marked in mph; in the Republic they are in kph.

Electricity

Republic 230V AC (50 cycles).
Northern Ireland 240V AC.
Plugs everywhere are the UK standard style with three square pins; two-pin round sockets may still be found in some parts of the Republic.

Embassies and consulates
Embassies in the Republic

Australia *Fitzwilton House, Wilton Terrace, Dublin 2. Tel: (01) 664 5300.*
Canada *65 St Stephen's Green, Dublin 2. Tel: (01) 417 4100.*
UK *29 Merrion Rd, Dublin 4. Tel: (01) 205 3700.*
USA *42 Elgin Rd, Ballsbridge, Dublin 4. Tel: (01) 668 8777.*

Consular Offices for Northern Ireland
Australian High Commission
Australia House, The Strand, London WC2B 4LA. Tel: (020) 7379 4334.
Canadian High Commission
Macdonald House, 1 Grosvenor Square, London W1X 0AB. Tel: (020) 7258 6600.
New Zealand Consulate
The Ballance House, 118a Lisburn Rd, Glenavy, Co Antrim BT29 4NY. Tel: (028) 9264 8098.

Practical guide

US Consulate *Danesfort House, 223 Stramillis Rd, Belfast BT9 5GR. Tel: (028) 9038 6100.*

Overseas embassies and consulates
Republic of Ireland
Australia *20 Arkana St, Yarralumla, Canberra 2600, ACT. Tel: (06) 214 0000.*
Canada *Suite 1105, 130 Albert St, Ottowa K1P 5G4. Tel: (613) 223 6281.*
New Zealand *7 Citigroup Bld, 23 Customs St East, Auckland. Tel: (09) 977 2252.*
UK *17 Grosvenor Place, London SW1X 7HR. Tel: (020) 7235 2171.*
USA *2234 Massachusetts Ave NW, Washington DC 20008. Tel: (202) 462 3939/42 (other consulates in several other cities).*

UK embassies and consulates (for Northern Ireland)
Australia *British High Commission, Commonwealth Ave, Yarralumla, Canberra. Tel: (02) 6270 6666.*
New Zealand *British High Commission, 44 Hill St, Thorndon, Wellington. Tel: (04) 924 2888.*
USA *British High Commission, 3100 Massachusetts Ave, NW, Washington DC. Tel: (202) 588 6500; UK Consulate, 845 3rd Ave, New York. Tel: (212) 752 8400.*

Emergency telephone numbers
Dial 999 for police, fire or ambulance services in both the Republic and Northern Ireland.

Health and insurance
Under an EU reciprocal arrangement, visitors from EU countries are entitled to medical treatment in both the Republic and Northern Ireland, but should obtain a European Health Insurance Card from their own National Social Security office. This should be

---

USEFUL WORDS AND PHRASES

Irish people are always pleased if visitors attempt a phrase or two in Irish. Here are a few words you may come across (along with how they are pronounced):

Irish	Pronunciation	English
ceilidh	*kaylee*	traditional dancing
Garda Siochana	*gawdasheekawnah*	police
tabhairne	*taw-er-nay*	pub
sláinte	*slawn-tay*	cheers
mas e do thoil e	*maws eh duh hull eh*	please
go raibh maith agat	*gurrah mah a-gut*	thank you
lá maith	*law mah*	good day
slán	*slawn*	goodbye
oiche mhaith	*ee-hay vah*	goodnight
céad míle fáilte	*kayed meela foilte*	welcome
mná	*manaw*	women (sign on toilets)
fir	*fir*	men (sign on toilets)

presented to the doctor if possible before treatment or a consultation starts. In the Republic you will need to make sure the doctor or dentist is registered with the Health Board before seeking treatment under the reciprocal arrangement.

Visitors from non-EU countries will need adequate medical insurance, and even EU citizens might be advised to seek additional cover. Medical insurance apart, a policy should include cover against third-party liability, lost baggage and trip cancellation. Make sure you keep all receipts to present with your insurance claim.

Travel insurance policies can be purchased through branches of Thomas Cook and most travel agents. Up-to-date health advice can be obtained from your Thomas Cook travel consultant.

Sometimes the choice can be overwhelming

Hitchhiking

As in other parts of the world, no place is totally safe for hitchhiking, especially for women. In the remoter parts of Ireland, hitching is the way the local people get around, but they are known to local drivers. Strangers may not be so lucky and might go a long time between lifts in places where the traffic is scant at the busiest of times. In Northern Ireland, hitchhikers may arouse suspicion among local people as well as the security forces.

Language

English and Irish are both official languages in the Republic and both are now taught in school. In the Gaeltacht areas of the west and north, Irish is likely to be the only language you will hear and it may be the only one on the signposts. However, you will always find someone who speaks English. (*See also box p180.*)

Lost property

Report serious losses – passport, credit cards, traveller's cheques – immediately. For lost passports, inform your embassy, which will be able to issue emergency documents. It may also be able to help with emergency funds if traveller's cheques are lost or stolen. (*See also* Money matters *pp182–3.*)

Maps and guides

Road maps of Ireland are freely available from car-hire companies, but for larger-scale regional and town maps the best map is the Ordnance Survey's

Skerries Mill in Co Dublin

Complete Road Atlas of Ireland. Town maps are usually available from local tourist offices and there is a host of guides for those with special interests, like Georgina Campbell's *Ireland for Garden Lovers.*

Media

The Republic's main newspapers are the *Irish Times, Irish Independent, The Examiner* and the tabloid *Star.* Sunday newspapers include the *Sunday Tribune* and the *Sunday Independent.* Provincial newspapers give a good insight into Irish life and reveal what is happening on the local entertainment scene.

The Republic has four television channels: RTE1, Network 2, TV3 and TG4 (the Irish-language channel). RTE stands for Radio Telefís Éireann, the state-owned broadcasting authority. UK radio and TV programmes can be received in most parts of Ireland.

In Northern Ireland the main daily newspaper is the middle-of-the-road evening *Belfast Telegraph.* The morning papers are the *Republican Irish News* and the *Loyalist News Letter.* Ulster TV is the regional commercial channel and the Province also receives programmes from the UK mainland and the Republic. The local BBC radio station is Radio Ulster and there are a number of independent stations.

Money matters

The euro (€) is the unit of currency in the Republic. There are seven denominations of the euro note: €5, €10, €20, €50, €100, €200 and €500; eight denominations of coins: 1 cent, 2 cents, 5 cents, 10 cents, 20 cents,

50 cents, €1 and €2. Northern Ireland uses sterling.

Banking hours in the Republic are 10am–4pm weekdays and until 5pm on Thursdays in Dublin and 5pm one day a week in other towns. Sub-branches in villages will probably be open only one or two days a week and may close for lunch. In Northern Ireland the main branches are open 9.30am–4.30pm, Monday to Friday, although some now open on Saturday too.

Currency and traveller's cheques can be exchanged at foreign exchange desks at the international airports on both sides of the border. Before exchanging at a bank it may pay to compare rates. Currency can also be exchanged at some post offices and tourist information offices. Hotels will also exchange currency and traveller's cheques. Major credit cards are accepted throughout the island in hotels, large department stores and major restaurants. In Northern Ireland, MasterCard and Visa are the most readily accepted cards.

If you need to transfer money more quickly, you can use the MoneyGram® Money Transfer service: *www.moneygram.com*

National holidays
(NI) Northern Ireland only
(R) Republic only
1 January New Year's Day
17 March St Patrick's Day
March–April, variable Easter Monday
First Monday in May May Day

Last Monday in May Spring Holiday (NI)
First Monday in June June Holiday (R)
12 July Orangemen's Day (NI)
First Monday in August
August Holiday (R)
Last Monday in August
Summer Holiday (NI)
First Monday in October
October Holiday (R)
25 December Christmas Day
26 December St Stephen's Day (Boxing Day)

Opening hours
Shops throughout Ireland are open generally 9am–5.30/6pm Monday to Saturday. Most shops also open for a shorter time on Sundays. Large shopping centres stay open until later on weekdays and open on Sundays. Some places have early closing on one day a week. In smaller towns and rural areas in the Republic, hours are more flexible and you may find that the general store may also be the local pub.

Pubs open in the Republic Mon–Thur 10.30am–11.30pm, Fri & Sat 10.30am–12.30am, Sun 12.30–11pm. At weekends, many pubs have extended opening hours. Northern Ireland's pub hours are 11.30am–11pm Mon–Sat with 30 minutes' 'drinking-up' time. Most pubs are open on Sun 12.30–1pm.

Organised tours
There is a wide range of organised tours of Ireland, mostly by coach.

There are 31 companies that are members of the Irish Incoming Tour Operators Association, which works closely with Bord Fáilte and the Northern Ireland Tourist Board. For information on guided tours in:
The Republic *CIE Tours International, 35 Lower Abbey St, Dublin. Tel: (01) 703 1888. www.cietours.ie*
Northern Ireland *Ulsterbus Travel Centre, European Buscentre, Belfast. Translink Call Centre. Tel: (028) 9066 6630.*

Cruising the Shannon can be an unusual way to see Ireland. River barges have been converted to give big-boat stability, luxurious accommodation and haute cuisine meals.

Cruises are offered by **Emerald Star** (*The Marina, Carrick-on-Shannon;* *tel: (071) 962 7633; www.emeraldstar.ie*) and **Shannon Cruisers** (*Williamstown Harbour, Whitegate, Co Clare; tel: (061) 927042; www.shannon cruisers.com*).

Dublin Sightseeing Tours (*tel: (01) 703 3028; www.dublinsightseeing.ie*) uses open-top buses and the 24-hour ticket allows you to hop on and off.

Another interesting city tour is the **Dublin Literary Pub Crawl**, in which actors guide groups round hostelries used by Beckett, Behan, Joyce and others – and the characters they created – and perform excerpts from their works (*tel: (01) 670 5602; www.dublin pubcrawl.com*).

Belfast has a narrated tour taking in the city's history and its most recent past, including the Shankhill and Falls

Ferries docked at Inisheer Harbour, Co Galway

Roads. Details from City Sightseeing Belfast (*tel: (028) 9032 1321; www.belfastcitysightseeing.com*).

Pharmacies

Cosmetics, feminine hygiene products and photographic film are stocked, as well as prescription and non-prescription drugs and medicines. Contraceptives, now legal throughout Ireland, may still be difficult to obtain in parts of the Republic. If closed, pharmacies display the address of the nearest one open.

Places of worship

Catholic and Protestant churches abound, but there are few non-Christian places of worship. Synagogues are to be found in Belfast, Cork and Dublin. Mosques can be found in Dublin.

Post offices

The Republic's post offices are open 9am–5.30pm Monday to Friday and 9am–1pm Saturday. Sub-post offices close at 1pm one day a week. The General Post Office in O'Connell Street, Dublin, is open 8am–8pm Monday to Saturday and 10am–6pm Sunday and public holidays. In Northern Ireland post offices are open 9am–5.30pm Monday to Friday and 9am–1pm Saturday.

Public transport

The *Thomas Cook European Timetable* has details of rail, bus and ferry times and can be bought from Thomas Cook branches in the UK, by telephoning (*01733) 416477*, or buy online at *www.thomascookpublishing.com*

Air

Flights from Dublin to other Irish airports are operated by Aer Lingus, Ryanair and Aer Arann. The Aran Islands receive flights from Inverin, Connemara, near Galway, by Aer Arann.

Bus

Bus Éireann (*tel: (01) 836 6111; www.buseireann.ie*) operates a network of express routes serving most of the country. Rover tickets offer a variety of 3- to 5-day travel passes offering unlimited travel on buses. **Dublin Bus/Bus Átha Cliath** (*tel: (01) 873 4222; www.dublinbus.ie*) serves the greater Dublin area. A 3- or 5-day Dublin Freedom ticket covers travel on the suburban rail network as well as all Dublin buses. **Ulsterbus Translink** (*tel: (028) 9066 6630; www.translink. co.uk*) runs an express link between Belfast and 21 Northern Ireland towns. Unlimited travel tickets are available. (*See* Impressions – Getting around *p26*.)

Ferry services

Licensed boat services operate from the mainland to some islands, weather permitting. The main services for the Aran Islands depart from Doolin or from Ros á Mhil in County Galway: *tel: (091) 568903; www.aranisland*

ferries.com; tel: (065) 707 4455; www.doolinferries.com; and tel: (065) 707 5949; www.mohercruises.com; Baltimore–Cape Clear (tel: (028) 28278; www.capeclearferries.com); Burtonport–Arranmore (tel: (074) 954 2233; www.arranmoreferry.com). See also www.irelandsislands.com

Two important car ferries run between Ballyhack, Co Wexford, and Passage East, Co Waterford (tel: (051) 382480/8; www.passageferry.ie), and Killimer, Co Clare and Tarbert, Co Kerry (tel: (065) 905 3124; www.shannonferries.com) (saving 100km/62 miles on the road journey). For ferries to Tory Island, tel: (074) 953 1320; www.toryislandferry.com; for Blasket Island, tel: (086) 335 3805; www.blasketislands.ie

Rail
Iarnród Éireann (tel: (01) 836 6222; www.irishrail.ie) and **Northern Ireland Railways** (tel: (028) 9066 6630; www.translink.co.uk) both offer special discounted rail tickets. The Irish Explorer gives unlimited rail travel for 5 out of 15 days throughout Ireland, and the Emerald Card covers island-wide bus and rail travel for various periods. (See Impressions – Getting around p26.)

Taxis
Taxis are available in major towns, at taxi stands or outside hotels, as well as at airports, main railway stations and ports. All cabs have meters, although you can negotiate fares outside main cities and airports.

Senior citizens
Customers over 50 or 55 can obtain discounts from many car-hire companies and from some hotels and tourist attractions. Several tour operators offer special spring and autumn packages for senior citizens.

Student and youth travel
Members of An Óige (Irish Youth Hostel Association) or the Youth Hostel Association of Northern Ireland (for addresses, see p169) can get discounts on some ferry crossings, and holders of a valid International Student Identity Card can buy a Travelsave Stamp, which entitles them to savings on main-line rail, long-distance bus and ferry services. Travelsave Stamps can be purchased from USIT, 19–21 Aston Quay, O'Connell Bridge, Dublin 2 (tel: (01) 602 1906). Travel throughout Ireland is allowed with a Eurail Youthpass, available only to those under 26 who live outside Europe. They can be purchased from travel agents but must be bought before the traveller leaves home.

Sustainable tourism
Thomas Cook is a strong advocate of ethical and fairly traded tourism and believes that the travel experience should be as good for the places visited as it is for the people who visit them. That's why we firmly support

The Travel Foundation, a charity that develops solutions to help improve and protect holiday destinations, their environment, traditions and culture. To find out what you can do to make a positive difference to the places you travel to and the people who live there, please visit *www.makeholidaysgreener.org.uk*

Telephones

Public telephones from which internal and international calls can be made are abundant. Phonecards are obtainable from post offices, newsagents and other shops. Most mobile phones will work in Ireland; check with your network operator if in doubt. The cheapest rates are between 6pm and 8am weekdays, and on weekends and public holidays. Calls made from hotel rooms are expensive.

Northern Ireland is part of the UK telephone system, so there are no special numbers for callers from the mainland to dial.

For international calls from Ireland, except Northern Ireland to Britain, dial *00*, followed by the country code:
Australia *61*
Canada and USA *1*
New Zealand *64*
UK *44*
Then dial the full number, omitting the first zero (does not apply to USA or Canada) of the area code.

In the Republic dial *10* for the operator, *11811* for directory enquiries within Ireland, *11818* for the international operator and *11818* for international directory enquiries, including Northern Ireland numbers.

In Northern Ireland dial *100* for the operator, *118500* for directory enquiries (including numbers in the Republic), *153* for international directory enquiries and *155* for the international operator. To ring Northern Ireland from the Republic, dial *048* followed by the telephone number.

Thomas Cook
Northern Ireland

A branch of Thomas Cook Travel can be found at: *10 Donegall Square West, Belfast. Tel: (0844) 335 7066.*

There are several more branches in Northern Ireland, including: *23 Kingsgate St, Coleraine. Tel: (0844) 335 7187.*

For up-to-the-minute details of Thomas Cook's travel and foreign money services, see *www.thomascook.com*

Time

Both the Republic and Northern Ireland follow Greenwich Mean Time (GMT), but with clocks put forward one hour from late March to late October. Time differences with other countries are:
Australia add 8 to 10 hours
Canada subtract 3½ to 8 hours
New Zealand add 12 hours
USA subtract 5 to 11 hours.

Tipping

Leave a tip of 10 to 15 per cent in hotels and restaurants. Keep in mind that some establishments include a service charge in the bill; ask about it. Taxi drivers expect 10 per cent of the fare and hotel porters €1 a bag.

Toilets

Public lavatories (in Irish *Fir* – Men, *Mná* – Women) are generally clean and serviceable at tourist locations.

Tourist offices

Tourism Ireland markets the Republic of Ireland and Northern Ireland abroad.

Australia *5th Level, 36 Carrington St, Sydney, NSW 2000.*
Tel: (02) 9299 6177.
Canada *2 Bloor St West, Suite 3403, Toronto ON M4W.*
Tel: (416) 925 6368.
South Africa *1st Floor, Southern Life Plaza, 1059 Schoeman St, PO Box 4174, Arcadia, Pretoria, South Africa 0083.*
Tel: (012) 342 5062.
UK *103 Wigmore St, London W14 1QS. Tel: (020) 7518 0800.*
USA *345 Park Ave, New York, NY 10154. Tel: (212) 418 0800.*

Bord Fáilte and the Northern Ireland Tourist Board provide tourist information on the island of Ireland.

There are 75 tourist information offices throughout the Republic and 26 tourist information centres in Northern Ireland. Dublin Tourism's main office is at the **Dublin Tourism Centre** at Suffolk Street (*tel: (01) 605 7700*). Northern Ireland Tourist Board's head office is at the **Belfast Welcome Centre** (*47 Donegall Place; tel: (028) 9024 6609*).

The **British Visitor Centre** (*1 Regent St, London SW1Y 4NS; tel: (020) 7493 3201*) also provides tourist information for Northern Ireland.

Travellers with disabilities

Facilities for visitors with disabilities are improving. Spaces are set aside in major car parks for vehicles carrying persons with disabilities, and an Orange Badge scheme allows drivers with disabilities on both sides of the border to park for free. Bord Fáilte uses the **Validated Accessible Scheme** to rate accommodation suitable for people with special needs, so look for the VAS accreditation. Wheelchairs may be hired from the **Irish Wheelchair Association** (*Blackheath Drive, Clontarf, Dublin 3; tel: (01) 818 6400; www.iwa.ie*). Its website includes an excellent list of links to sites that give advice and organise trips for wheelchair users.

For more information and help, contact: **Disability Action** (*189 Airport Rd West, Belfast BT3 9ED; tel: (028) 9029 7880; fax: (028) 9029 7881; www.disabilityaction.org*). See also *www.adaptni.org*, *www.dsni.co.uk* and *www.sharevillage.org*

Index

Acknowledgements

Thomas Cook Publishing wishes to thank the photographers, picture libraries and other organisations, to whom the copyright belongs, for the photographs in this book.

AA PHOTO LIBRARY pages 4, 24, 51, 52, 54, 57, 58, 60, 168, 169 (Michael Short); 15a, 30, 40, 43, 50 (G Munday); 18, 27, 75, 126 (J Blandford); 41, 76 (D Forss); 56 (L Blake); 73 (P Zoeller); 93 (Chris Hill); 124, 163 (Steffan Hill)
CONOR CAFFREY pages 6, 23, 32, 34, 69, 135, 175
DREAMSTIME.COM pages 1 (Winston Chang); 13 (Josemaria Toscano); 48 (Emeraldgreen); 59 (Lisa Riggs); 68 (Ron Sumners); 71 (Lpd 82); 77 (Pajda 83); 129 (Pavel Losevsky); 143 (Grgk); 184 (Gabriela Insuratelu)
FLICKR pages 28 (Nick L); 35 (Jan Zeschky); 36, 174 (William Murphy); 72 (mozzercork); 88 (Jimi Hughes); 103 (Jack Dawkins); 116 (Mike Mulligan); 119 (David Singleton); 132 (David Kinney)
PHOTOSHOT pages 85 (Ralph N Barrett); 86 (Designpics); 95 (World Pictures); 139 (Imagebroker.net)
SEAN SHEEHAN pages 16, 17, 26, 37, 61, 81, 84, 89, 110, 111, 113, 117, 138, 142, 145, 149, 166, 182
MICHAEL SHORT pages 14, 15b, 55
SPECTRUM COLOUR LIBRARY pages 7, 25, 39, 42, 64, 66, 74, 82, 90, 107, 109, 133, 134, 136, 151, 162, 167, 178, 181
TRAVEL PICTURES LTD pages 38 (Ken Walsh); 67 (George Munday); 141 (Charles Bowman); 147 (Stephen L Saks)

For CAMBRIDGE PUBLISHING MANAGEMENT LIMITED:
Project editor: Tom Lee
Typesetter: Julie Crane
Proofreaders: Jan McCann & Karolin Thomas
Indexer: Karolin Thomas

SEND YOUR THOUGHTS TO
BOOKS@THOMASCOOK.COM

We're committed to providing the very best up-to-date information in our travel guides and constantly strive to make them as useful as they can be. You can help us to improve future editions by letting us have your feedback. If you've made a wonderful discovery on your travels that we don't already feature, if you'd like to inform us about recent changes to anything that we do include, or if you simply want to let us know your thoughts about this guidebook and how we can make it even better – we'd love to hear from you.

Send us ideas, discoveries and recommendations today and then look out for your valuable input in the next edition of this title.

Emails to the above address, or letters to the traveller guides Series Editor, Thomas Cook Publishing, PO Box 227, Coningsby Road, Peterborough PE3 8SB, UK.

Please don't forget to let us know which title your feedback refers to!